CHRISTIAN HEROES: THEN & NOW

DAVID BUSSAU

Facing the World Head-on

CHRISTIAN HEROES: THEN & NOW

DAVID BUSSAU

Facing the World Head-on

JANET & GEOFF BENGE

YWAM
PUBLISHING
P.O. BOX 55787   SEATTLE, WA 98155

YWAM Publishing is the publishing ministry of Youth With A Mission. Youth With A Mission (YWAM) is an international missionary organization of Christians from many denominations dedicated to presenting Jesus Christ to this generation. To this end, YWAM has focused its efforts in three main areas: (1) training and equipping believers for their part in fulfilling the Great Commission (Matthew 28:19), (2) personal evangelism, and (3) mercy ministry (medical and relief work).

For a free catalog of books and materials, contact:

YWAM Publishing
P.O. Box 55787, Seattle, WA 98155
(425) 771-1153 or (800) 922-2143
www.ywampublishing.com

Library of Congress Cataloging-in-Publication Data

Benge, Janet, 1958–
David Bussau : facing the world head-on / Janet and Geoff Benge.
    p. cm.
  Includes bibliographical references.
  ISBN 978-1-57658-415-6
  1. Bussau, David. 2. Philanthropists—Australia—Biography. 3. Businessmen—Australia—Biography. 4. Opportunity International. I. Benge, Geoff, 1954– II. Title.
  HV28.B79B46 2008
  361.7′4092—dc22
  [B]   2008038539

David Bussau: Facing the World Head-on
Copyright © 2008 by YWAM Publishing

Second printing 2017

Published by Youth With A Mission Publishing
P.O. Box 55787
Seattle, WA 98155

ISBN-13: 978-1-57658-415-6; ISBN-10: 1-57658-415-1

Unless otherwise noted, Scripture quotations are taken from the Revised Standard Version of the Bible, Copyright 1946, 1952, 1971 by the Division of Christian Education of the National Council of the Churches of Christ in the U.S.A. Used by permission.

Printed in the United States of America.

CHRISTIAN HEROES: THEN & NOW

Available in paperback, e-book, and audiobook formats. Unit study curriculum guides are available for select biographies.

www.HeroesThenAndNow.com

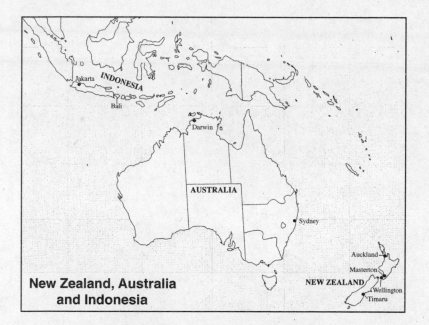

New Zealand, Australia and Indonesia

Contents

Chapter 1

A Grim Existence

Eight-year-old David Williams ran alongside the train as it rattled on the tracks. When he had matched his speed to the train's, he leaped up onto the side of a car that hauled coal, grabbed a metal bar, and quickly pulled his bare feet up until they came to rest on a ledge on the side of the coal car. He laughed as he did this; he loved the excitement of playing on a moving train. David's friend Wocky was already on the coal car and making his way along the side of it. David followed him.

"This is so much fun," David called out.

"Yeah," Wocky agreed. "But be careful. You know what happened to Billy."

David nodded. Billy was a year older than David. Three months before, he had slipped while leaping

11

up onto one of the freight cars, had fallen underneath it, and was killed as the car's metal wheels rolled over him. David was not going to let that happen to him. He made sure that his feet were firmly planted on the ledge, and he squeezed tight on the metal bar until his knuckles turned white.

When they reached the end of the coal car, the two boys slipped in between it and the boxcar behind. They clambered up onto the roof of the boxcar and crawled along. David felt the wind in his face as he watched Wocky make his way to the edge of the car and peer over. With his right hand, Wocky gave a thumbs-up signal. The door to the boxcar was open. Wocky disappeared over the edge of the boxcar as he swung himself in through the door. Moments later David plopped into the car beside him. Exhilarated, the two boys laughed aloud, their laughter echoing throughout the empty boxcar.

Suddenly the train lurched to a stop and then lurched again as it began heading in the opposite direction. As it moved back down the line, David walked over and poked his head out of the boxcar. His six-year-old brother Bruce was still standing beside the railway line. Then there was a loud clanging, and the train jerked violently as it connected to more freight cars. The jolt sent David sprawling to the floor as Wocky guffawed.

As the train came to a halt and prepared to head back the other way, Wocky said, "I have to go. It's time for dinner." With that he scrambled from the momentarily stationary train. David followed him.

The boys ran along the railway line, Bruce trailing in the distance, passing the black engine that belched steam and smoke. David heard the engineer yelling at him and Wocky. He couldn't actually make out the engineer's words, but he knew what they would be: "Don't you know that this is a dangerous place to play? And besides, unauthorized people are not supposed to be inside the railway yard, especially when an engine is shunting." But David didn't care. Playing on the shunting trains was about the most exciting thing there was to do in Moera, where David lived.

Moera was a tough, working-class neighborhood located in the Hutt Valley, just north of Wellington, New Zealand's capital city. Many of Moera's residents lived in uninviting, identical, government-supplied housing, like the three-bedroom house David lived in on York Street, which backed up onto the railway yard.

David's weatherboard house was grim from the outside, and life on the inside of it was even grimmer. David's mother, Marjorie, and three of his older siblings—sisters Margaret and Louise and brother John—lived in the house, along with his younger brother Bruce. David's father, Lewis Williams, had abandoned the family when David was very young, and David had no memory of the man. Yet he was aware of the fact that in the house there was often little to eat at mealtimes, and he usually went to bed feeling hungry. As well, the house brimmed with extra people, either visiting or staying for indefinite periods of time. And one of the things his mother and the extra people liked to do was sit around for hours on end, talking and drinking alcohol.

By now David had come to realize that when these people drank, things often got out of hand. Arguments would erupt that quickly turned violent. For their protection, David and his brother Bruce would often be hustled off to a bedroom by their mother or an older sister. The boys would hear yelling and screaming, and fists would soon fly. It was not uncommon for David to hear someone scrambling into the kitchen, searching for a carving knife with which to defend himself or herself or to attack someone else. David and Bruce would huddle together in the bedroom, sometimes for hours, until it was safe to come out again.

It was at times like these that David envied Wocky. For almost three years now Wocky had been living at the Anglican Boys' Home in the nearby town of Lower Hutt. He came home only during school vacations to stay with his grandmother, as he was doing now, spending the two-week May school holiday at home. At the boys' home, Wocky told David, there was always food to eat at mealtimes, and there were adults around who took an active interest in his life.

As Wocky talked, David thought about his experience at the Otaki Health Camp two summers ago. Otaki was located on the coast of New Zealand's North Island, about fifty miles north of his home. One of the purposes of the camp was to provide good nutrition to undernourished children. David had spent that summer gobbling down three healthy and plentiful meals a day and playing on the beach. But the thing that impressed him during his stay in Otaki was the fact that he was surrounded by adults who seemed to genuinely care about him. And the thing he secretly liked most was the new toothbrush he had been given when he arrived at the camp. Every time his housemother asked him if he'd brushed his teeth, David felt like he belonged somewhere at last. Back home in Moera he could go a week without using a toothbrush, or soap for that matter, and no one would notice.

David imagined that the boys' home, where Wocky lived most of the time, was a lot like the health camp, only it ran all year long. It sounded to him like a good life, especially since Wocky got to play all kinds of sports at the home and at school. David loved any kind of sport. He and Wocky would play endless games of cricket with the neighborhood boys on the empty lot beside Wocky's grandmother's house.

Much to David's disappointment, after two weeks at home, Wocky returned to the Anglican Boys' Home for the start of the winter term.

David also returned to school, and although he didn't much care for schoolwork, being at school meant escaping from the yelling at home. And during the lunch hour, some sort of sports game that he could join was always being played—be it rugby, soccer, cricket, or softball. Each morning David set out for school in bare feet, even on frosty mornings when the ground was crusted over with ice. His brother Bruce would trail along behind.

Then on Sunday, August 6, 1949, three months before David's ninth birthday on November 10, something happened that would change his life forever. It started out like most other Sundays, with David scrambling around in the kitchen looking for something to eat while the adults in the house slept off their hangovers. But around ten o'clock his mother got up and wordlessly went to the closet. She pulled out an old leather suitcase and headed for David and Bruce's bedroom. David followed her as she emptied the contents of their drawers into the suitcase. She then snapped the suitcase shut and told David to call Bruce and have them both put on their shoes. David was puzzled. Were they going somewhere? His mother wasn't dressed to go out, and she hadn't packed her own bag. Was someone else taking them on a holiday? He quickly dismissed the idea because his family never went away anywhere. But neither was it the right time of year for summer health camp. So where were they going?

When the suitcase was packed, David's mother told the two boys to follow her. Without saying a word, she led them to the nearby bus stop. David longed to ask his mother what was happening, but her look told him to keep his mouth shut.

The brothers waited with their mother at the bus stop for several minutes until an old bus rumbled to a halt in front of them. David's mother pushed the boys onto the bus and stepped onto the vehicle. She set the leather suitcase down beside David and turned to speak to the driver. "Drop these two off at the Anglican Boys' Home on High Street," she said as she handed over the fare. Without looking back, she stepped off the bus, which then pulled away from the stop. David looked over at Bruce. The two brothers sat staring at each other, unable to process what was happening to them.

As the bus made repeated stops to pick up and let off passengers, David tried to piece the situation together in his mind. Finally he concluded that the same social workers who had decided he should attend Otaki Health Camp had now decided that he and Bruce should live at the Anglican Boys' Home. But rather than being sad about this turn of events, David found himself getting excited as the bus made its way along. Wocky would be waiting for him, and every turn of the bus wheels was taking him farther away from the one place he hated most—home.

At last the bus hissed to a stop on High Street. "That's the boys' home there," the driver said, pointing to a large, old wooden house with a veranda on the front and a circular driveway.

David climbed down from the bus, lugging the leather suitcase with him. Bruce trailed behind. The bus pulled away from the curb, leaving the two boys in a belch of oily smoke.

"There's always something going on here. It's never boring. That's what Wocky reckons," David encouraged Bruce as they began to trudge up the gravel driveway.

As the boys approached the house, a heavyset, fearsome-looking woman who had short-cropped hair and was wearing an apron stepped onto the veranda. "And who might you two be?" she asked, with her hands on her hips.

"I'm David Williams, and this is my brother Bruce," David sputtered, unsure of the woman. Wocky had never told him that there was such a scary person at the boys' home.

"Ah, the Williams boys. We've been expecting you. I'm Miss Menzies, the matron of the home. Now come along inside."

David climbed the steps to the veranda and followed Miss Menzies inside, with Bruce close behind. The two boys soon found themselves standing in a long corridor with high ceilings that ran the length of the house, from which various doors opened to several rooms. The floor was so highly polished that David could see his reflection in it. An aroma wafted in through a side door. David sniffed deeply. *Smells like stew*, he told himself. *Stew and mashed potatoes. This place won't be so bad after all.*

Miss Menzies escorted the two boys to a nearby room. Neatly made bunk beds lined the walls. "This will be your room, Bruce," she said. "You stay here while I show your brother to his room."

David followed Miss Menzies on down the corridor, peering into doorways as he went. Each room had one purpose: one room was filled with concrete bathtubs, another with rows of toilets, and a third with only washbasins. David smiled to himself; cleanliness seemed to be important around here. Finally, at the rear of the house, Miss Menzies turned left into a large room with ten metal beds.

"This is where the older boys sleep," Miss Menzies said. "You can have that bed there." She pointed to a bed with two folded grey woolen blankets and a pillow stacked at the end. "Make your bed, put your things away in that locker, and then you can have a look around the place. The dinner bell rings at six o'clock. Don't be late. We do not accept tardiness here. Understand?"

"Yes," David said sheepishly as Miss Menzies turned and marched out of the room.

David pulled the blankets up over the hard kapok mattress and arranged the pillow, thinking about the day's turn of events. He wasn't sure whether he was lucky or unlucky to be at the boys' home. Yes, he was no longer around the volatile situation at home in Moera, but although Miss Menzies had been polite to him and Bruce, David could already tell that she was going to be a hard taskmaster.

After he had made his bed, David set out to explore his new home. Out front the lawn sprouted a stand of bamboo, and at the side of the house the lawn was wide and open. David walked across the lawn, feeling the spongy, close-clipped grass beneath his bare feet. As he rounded the corner of the house and headed into the backyard, he stopped in his tracks. He could scarcely believe his eyes. Right in the middle of the yard was a large swimming pool. David had never before seen a house with its own swimming pool. It was barely spring, but David imagined himself floating in the pool on warm summer afternoons.

Beyond the pool was a large garden stocked with all kinds of vegetables growing in neat rows. Behind the garden were fruit trees and a chicken coop full of squawking chickens.

This is an impressive place, David thought as he turned and headed back toward the house. Just then he heard the dinner bell ring, and not wanting to be late for his first meal at the home, he ran for the dining room. His stomach was already rumbling from hunger.

The dining room was paneled with kauri, a native wood noted for its fine grain, color, and toughness. Long tables covered in cream-colored tablecloths filled the room. The forty or so boys who lived at the home filed into the room, and each boy found a place at one of the tables. Miss Menzies and her assistant, Miss Adams, and any visitors sat at the top table.

"Hey, what are you doing here?" came a voice from behind. David recognized immediately that it was Wocky.

David shrugged his shoulders. "I don't know. My mum sent me and Bruce here," he replied.

As he spoke, Wocky burrowed into a place at the table beside David, who noticed Miss Menzies giving his friend a stern glance. But Wocky didn't seem to notice or care.

"This is great. We're going to have fun. We won't have to wait for the school holidays to play anymore," Wocky said as a plate of mutton stew was placed on the table in front of each boy.

David looked down at his plate. The food smelled delicious, but he just wished there were more of it on the plate. Didn't they realize he was famished?

Nonetheless, he reached for his knife and fork to begin eating, but Wocky reached out his hand and stopped him. "No, wait," he said.

David did as his friend told him. When a plate of stew had been placed in front of each boy, Miss Menzies rose to her feet. Instinctively the boys bowed their heads, and David followed their lead. Miss Menzies then recited grace, and at the end of the prayer, everyone in the room said "Amen" in unison. The dining room then erupted into a flurry of motion as the boys reached for their knives and forks and began eating their stew as fast as they could. Within moments David's plate was empty. He wished he could have some more, but none was offered. David resigned himself to still feeling hungry until breakfast, though he did wonder about Wocky's bragging that there was always plenty of food to eat.

After dinner, Wocky filled David in on life at the Anglican Boys' Home. "It's not going to be easy at first. You're going to get picked on because you're new, especially by that boy over there." Wocky pointed in the direction of a medium-built boy with dark brown hair sitting two tables away. "That's Ross Mense. He's a bully, and he'll pick on you for sure, so try to stay out of his way."

David nodded.

"We play all sorts of sports here after school and on the weekends. You're going to like it. And did you see the swimming pool? We use it all the time."

The next morning David discovered that Wocky had not been exaggerating about using the pool all the time. Despite the fact that it was cold outside and heavy dew lay on the lawn, at first light the boys were lined up naked and made to swim two lengths in the frigid water of the pool. David's teeth chattered as he waited to get into the pool. Wocky later told David that Miss Menzies believed that the morning swims would toughen the boys up. David hoped so. There had to be some payoff for being that cold so early in the morning.

After the morning swim, the boys dressed for school: khaki shorts and a grey shirt, which were supplied for David from a large box of hand-me-downs kept in the outdoor laundry. Then the boys headed to the dining room for breakfast, which consisted of a steaming bowl of oatmeal porridge. Next it was time for the homies, as the boys from the boys' home were called, to walk to nearby Eastern Hutt School for the day. Despite the fact that it was still bitter cold, none of the boys wore shoes.

After school David learned that an endless procession of chores had to be done around the house. The vegetable garden needed constant weeding, digging, and raking, while vegetables had to be peeled by hand for dinner. The chickens needed to be fed and fruit picked from the trees in the small orchard at the back of the property. And after dinner, a mountain of dishes had to be washed, dried, and put away.

Like most of the other boys, David liked best the job of polishing the linoleum floors in the house. The job occupied six boys, and after polish had been applied to the floor, three of the boys sat on an old blanket while the other three towed them along. With each succeeding pass, the surface of the linoleum was buffed to a gleaming luster. Sometimes the buffing got a bit rough as the boys hauling the blanket would hurl those on it into the walls.

After dinner and all the chores had been taken care of, it was time for homework. The boys would bring their books to the dining room, where Miss Menzies and Mr. Kimberly, the gardener, supervised them. David tried his best, but he found it hard to concentrate on schoolwork. He also quickly learned that Miss Menzies spent her time helping and praising those boys—among them Wocky—who seemed to have a natural aptitude for schoolwork, while she left the "underachievers" to themselves. It didn't take long for David to establish himself as an underachiever in order to be left alone.

It also didn't take David long to realize that Wocky had been right; it wasn't easy to fit in at the boys' home at first. Sure enough, Ross Mense picked on David, as did several of the other boys. David, though, stood his ground as best he could. Slowly the other boys began to accept him, especially when they discovered that he was a natural sportsman that they wanted on their team.

Things were tougher for Bruce, however. Bruce was small for his age, and no matter how much he combed his hair, it just seemed to stick straight out. The other boys teased him mercilessly about both his hair and his size. David wanted to help his little brother fit in, but so much of his energy was taken up trying to fit in himself that in the end he had to leave Bruce to fend for himself, which seemed to be the rule that each boy in the home lived by.

Several weeks after David and Bruce Williams arrived at the Anglican Boys' Home, they were summoned to Miss Menzies' office. David wondered whether it had something to do with his birthday. After all, he was turning nine in a few days. But when he and Bruce arrived at the office, they found their mother sitting in a chair.

"Boys, your mother is ready to have you back. Go pack your bags," Miss Menzies said. Their mother smiled nervously.

"Yes, I want you boys to come home. Things are better now. You'll see," Marjorie Williams chimed.

Before David realized it, words were flowing out of his mouth, words he had no idea he would say. "I'm not going home with you. I won't go back there. This is my home now."

"But David, everyone misses you. I promise things will be different. We went through a bad patch, but that's behind us now. You and Bruce must surely want to come home!" There was a pleading edge to his mother's voice. It made David feel guilty, but not guilty enough to give in. Now that he had said the words, he was not going to back down. There was no way he was going back to knife fights in the night and drunken brawls at home. No! Sometimes it was tough at the boys' home, but at least he felt safe there. The boys' home was where he was going to stay.

"I'm not going back there! Just leave me alone," David snapped as he glared at his mother. Then he turned and stormed out of the office, with Bruce right behind him. Little did David know at that moment that this would be the last time he would ever see his mother.

David Williams had a new home, the Anglican Boys' Home in Lower Hutt. That was where he now belonged.

Chapter 2

"Homie" Life

"This is God's house. He is here today. He hears each song we sing and listens when we pray to Him." With these words, which she intoned each Sunday morning, Mrs. Bonifant, a neighbor of the boys' home, called the Sunday school class to order. Sunday school was something new to David. Back in Moera his family had no time for church or religious activities. But David found he liked Sunday school, especially the lively singing and Bible stories Mrs. Bonifant told them. The whole thing was so much more exciting than the dreary services they attended at St. James Anglican Church every other week.

On this Sunday morning Mrs. Bonifant opened her Bible and read a passage from Psalm 27. As she read, the words of verse ten seized David's attention:

"For my father and my mother have forsaken me, but the LORD will take me up." David said the words over and over in his mind until he had memorized them. All week long he repeated the verse to himself and thought about what it meant. Yes, his mother had loaded him onto a bus and sent him off, and yes, his father had walked out on the family when David was a toddler. This verse clearly said that God would be his new Father and would look after him, no matter what. Deep inside, David relaxed. Things were going to turn out all right.

While David embraced God as his Father, at the boys' home he found in Miss Adams a nurturing mother figure. Miss Adams, an older woman with graying hair tied into a tight bun, came from a wealthy family and volunteered as an assistant at the boys' home. From the start David could tell that she wanted the best for the boys. Miss Adams was affectionate, encouraged them in all they did, and comforted them when they were hurt or depressed. At night she would read them bedtime stories.

From time to time, Miss Adams would also take a small group of boys on an excursion to her home. David loved the times when he got to go on these excursions. They would ride the train from Lower Hutt north up the Hutt Valley to Silverstream, where her large, two-story house was located. The house was surrounded by a croquet green, a tennis court, and an orchard. At her home, Miss Adams would serve the boys hot tea in huge white cups and give them two slices of homemade cake each. Best of all, she shooed them outside to explore her yard and orchard. The boys were allowed to eat all the fruit they wanted. David always felt sad when they had to leave her house and head back to the institutional routine of the boys' home.

While Miss Adams nurtured and encouraged the boys, Miss Menzies remained the strict disciplinarian. The rules of the home were to be obeyed, and if a boy did not keep to them, a heavy dose of punishment was meted out to him, usually in the form of a leather strap across the buttocks. Of course, David soon learned that no matter how hard you tried, at some point you would break one of the rules and incur Miss Menzies' wrath. But as his time at the boys' home went on, David, like the other boys, learned to take being strapped without flinching. As he discovered, however, not flinching while being punished could also lead to dire consequences.

Tony, one of the boys at the home, was caught talking during quiet time, an offense punishable by six strokes of the strap across his backside. As David would have done, Tony stood stone-faced and did not flinch as Miss Menzies gave him six swift strokes with the strap. This time, the fact that Tony did not flinch seemed to enrage Miss Menzies. David and the other boys watched in horror as she gave him six more whacks with the leather strap. And when Tony still did not flinch, she gave him six more whacks. It wasn't until he had received twenty-one hits with the strap that Tony finally broke into sobs. Tony's backside and the top of his legs were crisscrossed with a mass of red welts that were so painful he was forced to lie facedown on his bed while Miss Adams tried to comfort him.

News of the vicious strapping eventually reached the vicar of St. James Anglican Church, who oversaw the boys' home. The vicar paid Miss Menzies a visit in her office. The two of them had a heated exchange of words. After the visit, news spread among the boys that the vicar had forbidden Miss Menzies from using the leather strap to punish them. David, like the others, breathed a sigh of relief. Sadly, the boys' change in fortune didn't last. Four days later Miss Menzies was so frustrated that she again picked up her leather strap, and the beatings continued.

Despite the threat of harsh punishment, David found lots of good times at the home. On the weekends the boys had free time to play, when David's sports prowess was allowed to shine. They would gather on the playing field next to the house and play endless games of cricket, rugby, and soccer.

One of David's other favorite activities was building forts in the enormous pile of wood used to fire the stove in the kitchen and the coppers used to boil water for the laundry. David and some of his friends would pull out pieces of wood and restack them until they had created a kind of cave in the middle of the wood pile, and then they would climb in and play make-believe games. The results of their fort-building efforts were not always secure, and on more than one occasion the whole woodpile collapsed on David, leaving him battered and bruised.

On warm summer afternoons, the boys were allowed to play in the swimming pool, where they would float in inner tubes and splash and chase each other in the water. The pool had just one problem: no filtration system. Instead, it was filled from an artesian well on the property, and with no chemical additives, the water slowly became murky and green. Finally, when the water was so bad that the boys emerged tinged with green from the algae, the pool was emptied. Then the boys had the backbreaking task of scrubbing every inch of it clean before it was refilled. David didn't mind the effort of having to scrub the pool on a regular basis. To him it was worth it for the luxury of having a swimming pool to play in.

David learned that many of the boys in the home had secret hiding places, and he decided to find his own hiding place. One night after the lights went out, David climbed out of bed and sneaked into the yard. He counted off six paces from the back door, turned to his right, and counted off eight more paces. At this spot he took out a small knife he had "borrowed" from the kitchen and cut out a square of sod, removing it carefully. He then dug out several handfuls of dirt to make a hole big enough in which to place a tobacco tin, and then he replaced the sod. This was now his secret hiding place where he planned to hide any money he found, since the boys were not allowed to keep any money on them.

When he had stashed several pennies, or perhaps a threepence or a sixpence, David would sneak out at night and retrieve some of the money from his secret hiding place. He would make sure that no one was watching him, and then he would cross the road to the store to buy a bag of candy or some broken cookies, which he would gobble down as fast as he could before heading back to his room and quietly hopping back into bed. His full stomach and the small adventure gave him a feeling of power, and that feeling was worth the risk of being caught—and punished.

Four months after David had arrived at the boys' home, it was time to get ready for Christmas. David heard lots of talk about a Christmas party at Clouston's mill. Arthur Clouston was the owner of a successful sawmilling business and had himself grown up in an orphanage. As a result, he now did whatever he could to help children in need throughout the Hutt Valley region. He was the person who donated the huge pile of firewood that David liked to build forts in.

Finally the day of the party arrived, and Miss Menzies told the boys to line up outside. Excitement mounted as two flatbed trucks from the sawmill pulled up in front of the home. The boys, along with Miss Menzies and Miss Adams, climbed onto the back of the trucks and held on tightly to each other. The trucks headed eighteen miles north up the Hutt Valley, where they turned onto a branch road that led up the Akatarawa Valley.

The road was narrow and winding, and more than once David thought he might be thrown from the back of the truck as it lurched around a sharp bend. The road wound along the side of a narrow river gorge and then finally descended into the upper reaches of the Akatarawa Valley. There on an open stretch of flat land beside the river sat two rows of houses in which the mill workers lived. Beyond the houses was the sawmill.

The two trucks pulled onto an open grass field bounded on one side by the sawmill and on the other by the river. Mr. Clouston enthusiastically welcomed his guests, and soon several more trucks arrived bringing children from other orphanages to the event. Before long the field was alive with children laughing, playing, sack racing, three-legged racing, egg-and-spoon racing, and chasing a greased pig.

David had never had so much fun before, and things only got better when he heard the sound of an airplane buzzing overhead. He looked up to see a red biplane circling above the field. As the plane circled, it let loose a flood of candy that crashed to the ground like hail in a storm, only this hail was sweet and delicious. Soon David was scurrying around try-ing to scoop up as much of the candy as he could before the other children got to it. In truth there was more candy than any one child could collect and eat. Like David's, the pockets of the other children bulged with candy.

As if that were not enough, Mr. Clouston called everyone to the tents that were set up at the end of the field. There laid out for his guests was a feast of sausage rolls, sandwiches, and cream cakes. The sight of so much food was like a dream come true to

David. And an endless supply of lemonade flowed with which to wash down all the goodies. David ate and drank until his stomach ached and he was forced to sit down for a few minutes to rest and let all the food and candy settle.

Finally the party was over and it was time to leave. David climbed onto the truck for the journey back to the boys' home, carrying with him lots of memories to relive in the days to come.

Life continued on at the home, with the annual Christmas party being the biggest and best event every year. But David could not stay at the home forever. By September 1953, he was only two months from turning thirteen. Four years after arriving at the Anglican Boys' Home in Lower Hutt, David Williams once again found himself on a bus. He was leaving the home behind and heading for Masterton, a town located sixty miles north on the expansive Wairarapa Plains. Located at Masterton was Sedgley Boys' Home for teenage boys, also run by the Anglican Church.

At Sedgley, David was reunited with Wocky, who had transferred to the home the year before. Wocky was able to help David get oriented to his new surroundings, just as he had done in Lower Hutt.

Sedgley Boys' Home was situated on twenty-five acres of land on the edge of Masterton. A large house that sat on the property contained dormitories for the boys, a dining room and kitchen, and quarters for the home's supervisor. Like the boys' home in Lower Hutt, the house was surrounded by flower gardens and expansive stretches of lawn where the boys could play various games. And like the Lower Hutt home, Sedgley had its own swimming pool where the boys took an early morning swim. It also had a large, fully equipped gymnasium, along with a workshop and a milking shed and dairy. It had a much larger chicken coop and acres of vegetable garden. As Wocky explained to David, the place was pretty much self-sustaining and there were always plenty of vegetables, butter, and cheese to eat, along with fresh milk to drink. But as David soon discovered, being self-sustaining meant that there were plenty of chores that needed to be done each day.

The day he arrived at Sedgley, David was instructed to report to the kitchen at five-thirty the following morning to help prepare breakfast and then wash and put away the dishes. Helping in the kitchen would be his chore for the next three months. Other boys were milking the cows, separating the milk and cream in the dairy, doing the laundry, or tending to the vegetable garden. The boys had hardly a moment to spare, and any spare minutes were filled with trying to secure a place in the pecking order of the home.

Before leaving the boys' home in Lower Hutt, David had been one of the older boys. He was looked up to and respected by the younger boys at the home. But because David was one of the youngest boys at Sedgley, he had to set about establishing his place in the order of things. In particular this meant once again contending with Ross Mense, the bully from the Anglican Boys' Home who had come to Sedgley two years before. At Sedgley Ross was an even bigger bully, ordering the younger boys to make his bed, clean his shoes, and even do his chores. It wasn't long before Ross zeroed in on David and tried to bully and intimidate him into doing things for him. But David had decided he was not going to give in to bullying. When Ross tried to get David to clean his shoes for him, David flatly refused.

"If you don't, I'm going to beat you up," Ross countered.

"Well then, you'll have to beat me up, because I'm not cleaning your shoes," David replied determinedly.

That is exactly what Ross did, beating David till his nose bled. But still David held firm, and the frustrated bully stormed off.

On several more occasions Ross tried to bully David by beating him up. But with each beating, David's resolve not to give in grew stronger. David reasoned that eventually Ross would tire of expending so much energy in his bullying efforts and give up on David. That is exactly what happened. Soon a smoldering stalemate developed between David and Ross, and the bully moved on to look for other boys to do his chores for him. David's stand against Ross earned him the respect of most of the other forty boys at Sedgley.

By the time David had celebrated his thirteenth birthday, he was feeling quite at home at Sedgley Boys' Home, and he looked forward to all that life had in store for him.

Chapter 3

Life in Masterton

"Come and look at this," one of the boys called excitedly.

David and five other homies were on their way to St. Matthew's Anglican Church to attend Sunday school, and they ran to see what the boy had found.

Lying in the street was a single bullet.

"Let's pelt it with stones and see if it'll go off," one of the homies suggested.

David gathered up a handful of stones from the side of the road and gathered round the bullet with the other boys. Then each boy took a turn hurling a stone at the bullet. As David soon discovered, the bullet wasn't easy to hit with a stone. Finally, a stone thrown by one of the homies connected with the bullet, causing a loud crack and a puff of smoke. The boys cheered with delight.

At the same moment, David felt his leg start to sting. He looked down and saw blood flowing from a gash in his thigh, which had been grazed by the bullet. He watched the faces of the other boys go ashen when they saw what had happened. By now the pain was intense, and David unbuttoned his shirt and took off his undershirt, which he tied tight around his thigh to try to stop the bleeding.

Once the undershirt was securely in place and David had rebuttoned his shirt, the boys continued on their way to Sunday school, David hobbling along as best he could on his injured leg. There was no thought of heading back to Sedgley. That would only get them into more trouble. Instead, David sat through Sunday school in agony, trying to think up a story to explain his wound. Finally he decided he would tell Mr. Jonkers, the current master at Sedgley, that he had fallen on the way home from Sunday school and cut his leg. After Sunday school, he told the story to the other boys, who all agreed to stick to it.

"You can't have gotten that wound from simply falling over," Mr. Jonkers said in his Dutch-accented English when David unwrapped the undershirt from his wound.

"Yes, sir, I did," David protested.

Mr. Jonkers gave him a disbelieving look and questioned the other boys, who all agreed that David had fallen on the way home and cut his leg.

David breathed a silent sigh of relief when they all stuck by his story, but then he shouldn't have been surprised. Not ratting out another homie, no matter what, was the credo the boys at Sedgley lived by. If Mr. Jonkers had found out just how David had injured his leg, he certainly would have punished the boys severely for their stupidity.

Soon the wound on David's thigh healed, and David was back into the routine of life at Sedgley. He was kept busy with chores and attending school, yet he still had time to play various games of sport with the other boys on the lawn surrounding the main house. As usual, David excelled in whatever sport the boys played. He also became accomplished in something else—gymnastics. Each Tuesday night, Stan and Rex Tatton, brothers who had been New Zealand gymnastic champions, came to Sedgley and taught the boys gymnastics. David eagerly awaited their arrival, and he quickly proved himself adept at the sport. He learned to tumble on the mats and vault over the horse, but most of all he liked the parallel bars and the Roman rings. On these two pieces of equipment he would push his agility and upper-body strength to their limits.

Bicycles played a big part in the lives of the boys at Sedgley. Since owning his own bike gave a boy a measure of independence, David decided that he needed a bike. The Sedgley boys' bikes were not bought from a store; that was not in the budget. Instead the bikes were built from old parts salvaged from the local dump. David made several trips to the dump, where he found old bicycle wheels and a twisted bike frame.

Once he had collected enough bike parts, David set to work in the workshop at Sedgley, beating the buckles out of the wheel rims and putting new spokes in them. He then straightened the front forks and the rest of the frame before sanding and painting it. However, he hadn't been able to find a few parts at the dump or among the pile of old bike parts at the back of the workshop. To get these parts, David turned to another misguided credo of the boys at Sedgley: steal what you need. He stole a seat from a bike parked at school and the handlebars from another bicycle left outside the local cinema. Before long he had built himself a bike and was soon riding all over town.

Now that he had one bike, David decided that he had enough parts—or could "acquire" enough parts—to build a faster, more stripped-down bike to use when he raced the other boys on the bike track on the Sedgley grounds. However, David soon found himself on the receiving end of the stealing credo, as the other boys stole parts from whatever bike he wasn't using at the time.

The Sedgley boys had a whole range of late-night adventures, which began soon after the lights went out. When they were sure the coast was clear, each boy pushed his pillow under his blanket to create a boy-sized hump and then quietly slipped out the dorm window. Some nights the boys would ride their bikes to one of the orchards that dotted the outskirts of Masterton and raid it, piling as many apples, pears, or peaches as they could fit into their pillowcases, and then ride back to Sedgley. Once home, the boys would head for one of the underground forts they had constructed on the edge of the property and feast on their "booty."

David had another booty he liked to feast on—cookies. He and several of the other boys had found a way into the back of a nearby grocery warehouse. David would scramble up the back wall of the warehouse and then squeeze through the gap at the top of it, just below the roof. Then he would carefully lower himself down and stuff as many packets of chocolate cookies as he could fit down his sweater before escaping back the way he had come, being careful not to crush the pilfered cookies. Once back at Sedgley, another feast would ensue in one of the boys' forts. However, this activity came to a halt when the owners of the warehouse discovered how the thief was getting in and plugged the hole at the top of the wall.

And then there was Spooky Bill. This was basically a game of hide-and-seek played in the darkened gym. The catch to the homies' version of the game was that they played it not on the floor of the gym but rather in the rafters, high above the floor. This injected an exciting and dangerous element into the game. In fact, it was not uncommon for someone to slip and fall to the floor, breaking an arm or a leg in the process. Of course, if the boys were caught playing this dangerous game, it would mean swift punishment from the master, both for being out after lights-out and for engaging in such a dangerous activity. As a result, whenever someone fell, the other boys would carry him back to the dorm, slide him through the window, and arrange him in his bed. The boy would suffer in silent agony through the night, and in the morning it would be reported that he had fallen out of bed and injured himself. David decided that Mr. Jonkers probably thought he had New Zealand's most accident-prone group of sleepers under his care.

After completing elementary school, David began attending the local high school, Wairarapa College, located just a few streets from Sedgley. As in elementary school, he struggled with classroom work, but he more than made up for his mediocre academic performance with sports. Once again he excelled, playing on the college's cricket team in the summer and on the soccer, rugby, and hockey teams during the winter months.

During summer vacation, David liked to work to earn money. In his first summer at Sedgley he worked on a farm about ten miles south of Masterton, in Carterton, where he dug potatoes from the field and placed them into sacks. This was hot, back-breaking work as he hunched over all day long. At night, when he stretched out to sleep in the barn, his body ached. To David this was a minor inconvenience. He liked to work hard and tried to do the best job he possibly could, hoping to beat the expectations of his employer along the way. For another summer vacation, David worked at an orchard in Featherston, twenty-five miles south of Masterton.

On the weekends the boys were allowed to do odd jobs around the neighborhood to earn money. David liked to mow lawns, and he would canvass the neighborhood, offering his services. However, it wasn't always easy to convince a homeowner to let David mow his or her lawn, especially when the homeowner learned that David was a homie from Sedgley. The Sedgley boys' reputation as petty thieves preceded them, and most people did not want the boys anywhere near their homes. But on those occasions when someone let him mow the lawn, David did the best job possible in the hope that the person would pay him well and invite him back to mow it again. He also tried his best not to steal from the people who hired him, though he couldn't seem to help himself whenever he spotted a pack of cigarettes left unattended. He would scoop them up into his pocket, and at night after lights-out, he and several of his friends would sneak out to their fort and smoke them.

When he was fourteen, rather than spend his vacation laboring on another farm, David decided to take a job at Donalds, a local company that manufactured wool presses used on farms to compress freshly shorn fleeces from sheep into tight bales for shipping. The pay was much better than any of his previous jobs, and that appealed to David.

Wocky also went to work at Donalds, and on their first day of work, he and David rode their bikes together to the factory. The foreman shook their hands and welcomed them, saying, "Rob [as Wocky now preferred to be called], I'll put you to work in the engineering area. And David, you'll be upstairs in the carpentry shop."

And so David found himself upstairs guiding lengths of timber across the spinning circular blade of a table saw to produce the various-sized pieces of wood needed to build the wool presses. The spinning, jagged blade of the saw had no safety guard over it, and it spewed sawdust into the air as it bit its way through the wood. David would hold the timber firmly against the guide with his hand and carefully feed it forward through the blade. It was precise work, and David enjoyed the challenge of getting it perfect.

Several weeks after starting work at Donalds, David was feeding a length of timber through the saw when the blade caught on a knot in the wood. In an instant the wood violently jerked up, dislodging David's left hand from its grip and flinging his hand toward the blade. David became aware of a strange stinging sensation in his fingers, and he quickly pulled his hand aside. When he held up his hand to see what had happened, he saw four bleeding stumps where his fingers had been. His thumb had also been cut through and was dangling by a piece of skin. Instinctively David ripped off his shirt and wrapped it around his mangled hand as he called out, "Help me."

David's coworkers came running to his aid. When they saw what had happened, two of them quickly rummaged through the pile of sawdust under the saw and were able to find two of David's severed fingers. They dropped the two fingers into a plastic bag and rushed David to the hospital. By now David was feeling faint from the loss of blood and from the realization of what had happened to him. And the stinging he had felt at the time of the accident had now turned into an excruciating, throbbing pain.

At the hospital, David was given anesthetic. When he came to he was lying in bed with his left hand bound in a mass of white gauze bandages. He was relieved that at least the pain seemed to have gone. He tried to focus his bleary eyes on the nurse as she explained that a surgeon had been able to reattach his thumb and index and middle fingers, but David's ring finger and little finger now ended at his first knuckle. As David tried to comprehend what the nurse had just told him, he slipped from consciousness.

It wasn't until the next day when David awoke that he fully grasped the reality of the situation. His mind was immediately filled with questions. Would he be able to use his hand again? How would it affect his life? And more important, how would it affect his ability to play sports? Most of his sporting endeavors required the use of his hands to catch and throw balls. How could you catch a cricket ball if you were missing fingers?

"Will I be able to play cricket again?" David finally asked the nurse one day.

"You'll be fine," the nurse reassured him. "Your fingers won't look pretty, but they'll eventually work again. You'll be back playing cricket before you know it. Of course you're never going to be able to play the piano or the guitar, but other than that you'll do just fine."

David tried to be encouraged by her words, but he had his doubts. As the lingering effects of the anesthetic wore off, the pain returned, and his fingers began to throb. As he lay in his hospital bed, David practiced strategies to help him deal with the pain. He finally trained his mind to dull the pain he was feeling and repress the images of the accident that kept replaying in his mind.

Despite the fact that he was recovering from a serious injury to his hand, David found himself enjoying his time in the hospital. The individual care and attention he received from the nurses was something he had never before experienced in his life. The nurses seemed to really care about him, and he enjoyed passing the time talking with them and flirting with the pretty, young nurses.

Finally after three weeks in the hospital, David returned to Sedgley. He was sad to have to leave the hospital and all the encouragement he received from the nurses. And he noticed the contrast at Sedgley right away. The other boys didn't seem to care that he was back, and they showed little interest in the details of his accident. Despite his injury, David was soon put back on the duty roster. Of course, he could no longer milk the cows, and the risk of getting an infection in his injured hand meant he didn't have to wash the dishes. However, David did soon learn to do most of the other chores adequately.

David also was able to play sports again. At first this consisted of playing soccer, which required only the use of his feet. As his fingers continued to heal and become more flexible, he found that he could catch and throw a cricket ball. Before long, he was once again playing cricket for Wairarapa College. However, the injury did curtail his gymnastics. He could still vault and tumble, but without two fingers on his left hand, he no longer had the grip necessary for the parallel bars and Roman rings.

Losing two fingers brought David an unexpected influx of money. One day, Mr. Hills, the new master at Sedgley, called him to his office and explained that the government was going to pay David two thousand pounds' compensation for losing his two fingers. "I'll arrange to have the money deposited into a trust fund for you. You won't be able to spend it until you're eighteen."

David left Mr. Hills's office stunned. Two thousand pounds was a lot of money, and it still would be in four years, when he would be allowed to spend it.

Back at Wairarapa College, classwork continued to be a challenge for David. He liked his metal work, woodwork, and technical drawing classes, but math, science, and English were excruciatingly boring, especially English. In fact, the homies in the class took every opportunity they could to escape from English class. Whenever Mr. Mountford, their teacher, turned to write on the blackboard, David or one of the other homies would climb out through the classroom window and hide under the school building for the rest of the period. No one really seemed to care that the boys did this, and Mr. Mountford never came looking for them. David knew why this was: they were homies, and no one expected much from the homies. He knew that most people thought they were juvenile delinquents who would most likely end up in jail when they finished school. The only place the homies were respected at Wairarapa College was on sports teams, where they were often star players with a reputation for toughness.

David also knew that all the boys at Sedgley were aware of the community's perception of them—boys who probably wouldn't amount to much in life and, if they did manage to stay out of jail, would most likely end up as laborers on a farm or a building site somewhere. This, however, didn't stop the boys from having dreams, which they sometimes talked about together. One day as David and several of the other homies were in the workshop making repairs to their bikes, they talked among themselves about life after Sedgley.

"I'm going to buy a farm and marry a beautiful wife," one of the boys said.

"I'm going to move to Auckland and find a good job there," said another.

"And I'm going to land a job in an office somewhere. You wait and see," added another boy.

David listened to what the others said and thought for a few moments. He didn't often talk to the other boys about what he was thinking, but this time he opened his mouth and said, "I'm going to be a millionaire and retire by the time I'm forty!"

The other boys stopped what they were doing and stared at David, who could scarcely believe the words he had just spoken. Yet deep down inside he knew that he could do it. He didn't know how, but one day he was certain that he would be a millionaire. Time would tell.

Chapter 4

A New Beginning

Hot dogs! Hot dogs! Get your hot dogs here."
David was on his way to watch a visiting team play the local Masterton rugby team at Solway Showground, located about two blocks from Sedgley. He had been to the venue to watch many rugby games before, and on those occasions he had not particularly noticed the vendor selling hot dogs from a stand outside the main grandstand. But today, something about the rhythmic way the man called out to the crowd attracted David's attention. David stopped for a while and watched the hot dog vendor at work. As he watched, he began to think that this was something he could do, something that combined two important things for him—his love of sports and the need to earn some money.

"Would you be willing to rent me a stand?" David finally asked the hot dog vendor.

The man gave David a long, sideways glance.

"I think this is something I could be good at," David added.

"You do, do you?" said the vendor.

David nodded.

Before long, David had worked out an arrangement with the hot dog vendor. The vendor would provide him with a stand from which to sell hot dogs, and in return, David would pay him a portion of all the money he made. The next time a rugby game was held at Solway Showground, David was there with his hot dog stand, eagerly selling hot dogs to people as they flooded into the grandstand.

David was amazed at how easily things went and at how much money he was able to make, even after he had paid the vendor his commission. It was not nearly as hard as mowing lawns or milking cows. Within a month he had arranged for a second hot dog stand. He recruited one of his friends from Sedgley to man the stand and collected a share of his profits, which he kept for himself. At the end of three months, David had three hot dog stands at the showground. The whole enterprise was a revelation to David. It might not make him a million pounds, but the experience showed him that he seemed to have an innate feel for business.

While David was successful with his hot dog stand endeavor, he continued to struggle along academically at high school. No matter how hard he tried, schoolwork was difficult. But away from the classroom, on the sports field it was a different matter. David played on Wairarapa College's cricket, rugby, and soccer teams, where he excelled.

When David arrived at Sedgley from Boys' Home in Lower Hutt, Mr. and Mrs. Jonkers managed the place. When the Jonkerses moved on, Mr. and Mrs. Hills replaced them. The Bakers followed Mr. and Mrs. Hills. Most of the time, the Bakers reeked of liquor, and each time Mr. Baker weaved his way unsteadily down the corridor, word spread that the couple were alcoholics. As a result, the Bakers did not last long at Sedgley. In 1956 Lyndsay and Vera Bussau and their five-year-old daughter, Rochelle, arrived to take the Bakers' place.

The Bussaus had a more relaxed management style than their predecessors, choosing to selectively enforce the rules that governed the boys' behavior at Sedgley. David noticed that his friend Wocky, or Rob, was one of the first to benefit from this more relaxed approach. Because it was against the rules for the boys at Sedgley to have a girlfriend, Rob had been secretly dating Diane, an attractive girl from Wairarapa College. He would sneak off after the lights went out to see Diane. But with the Bussaus running Sedgley, Rob was now allowed to go to Diane's house for lunch on Sundays. David envied Rob. He would like to have a girlfriend, and he secretly admired Dorothy Bell, a girl in one of his classes at school. But while he found her attractive, he lacked the confidence to talk to her. Besides, he was a Sedgley boy, he would tell himself, and everyone knew that Sedgley boys were the lowest of the low. Why would a girl like Dorothy Bell be interested in him?

One day David found Rochelle Bussau, or Rocky, as most people called her, sitting and playing with some blocks. He asked her what she was making.

"I'm making a house," Rocky replied with pride.

"Here, let me help you," David said as he sat down beside her.

Even David was impressed by the end result. It was interesting, and Rocky seemed delighted with it. She insisted on dragging her mother out to admire it.

Then, several days later, when the chain came off Rocky's bike, David wheeled the bike around to the workshop and repaired it for her. He watched as Rocky pedaled off on the bike when he was done, waving back at him as she went.

David had to admit that he was growing rather fond of Rocky. He began to treat her like a little sister, and he sensed that Rocky liked him, too, seeking him out to talk and play with her. And David would oblige whenever he could.

The Bussaus noticed the little sister/big brother relationship that had developed between David and their daughter. Soon David found himself being invited to the Bussaus' quarters, where he would hang out and play with Rocky while Vera Bussau served him tea in a china cup and plied him with cookies. David enjoyed these times in the Bussaus' quarters. The family had a closeness that he had never felt in his own family back in Moera. David felt valued, and he felt that the Bussaus really cared about him.

During these times, however, David noticed a few things about the Bussaus. Vera Bussau, a short, rotund woman, ruled the roost. She was always telling her husband, Lyndsay, a lanky man with glasses and a bushy mustache, what to do, and she could become very angry very quickly when he failed to follow her instructions.

Despite these observations, David continued to enjoy the time he spent with Lyndsay, Vera, and Rocky. In fact, he looked forward to spending time with them, even when the other boys ribbed him about the cozy, favored relationship he had forged with the new managers.

During 1956, David's name was added to the Sedgley Honor Board. Each year the name of the boy deemed the best at the home was inscribed on the board. David felt a strange pride when he saw his name on the board. He knew it wouldn't seem like much to the other boys in his class at school, but within the system at Sedgley, it was quite an honor. It reinforced to David that by working hard and applying himself, he could make a difference in the daily lives of those around him.

As 1957 rolled around, David entered his final year of high school. As usual, he continued to struggle in the classroom. The only thing that excited him at school was sports. By now, with all the physical activity he had been involved in over the years, he had developed into a solid, muscular young man, talented in multiple sports. As a result, during his final year David served as the captain of the Wairarapa College First XI cricket team in the summer and captain of the school's top soccer team during the winter. It was a great honor, and even though he was a homie from Sedgley, students at Wairarapa College looked up to him. David savored his achievement.

One day during 1957, Lyndsay Bussau called David aside to talk.

"David," Lyndsay began, "I've accepted a job as a teacher, and Vera, Rocky, and I are going to be moving shortly down to Timaru. We were wondering if you'd like to come and live with us there."

At first David was shocked to hear that the Bussaus were leaving Sedgley, but then he was delighted—and honored—that they wanted him to come and live with them. Not only was he in his last year of high school, but also he was in his last year of living at Sedgley. At the end of the year he would be expected to move out on his own, find a job, and build a life for himself outside the institutional setting he had lived in for the past eight years. What the Bussaus were offering David was a sense of belonging as he moved into this next phase of his life, a place where there would be people around who he believed truly cared about him as a person.

"Yes! I'd love to come with you to Timaru," David replied.

It was agreed that David would finish the year at Wairarapa College and then travel to Timaru to join the Bussaus.

"Have a good trip," David told Rocky as the Bussau family set out for Timaru.

"I'm going to miss you," Rocky replied.

"You know I'll be down there with you soon," David said.

Throughout the rest of the year David daydreamed about what it was going to be like living with a normal family, and he eagerly awaited the start of his new life.

As the end of the year approached, David began making plans for the move south to Timaru. He didn't have much to take with him, mostly clothes, a few books, and the experience of having grown up in an orphanage, some of which had been good and some bad.

Finally the school year was over, and David said good-bye to the boys at Sedgley and left his life in Masterton behind. He was on his way to Timaru, located midway down the east coast of New Zealand's South Island. He took a bus south from Masterton to Wellington, where he spent a few days exploring the city. Then he caught an overnight ferry to Nelson, at the top of South Island. From there he caught another bus that would take him to Timaru.

As the bus headed south, David made an important decision. His early family life in Moera and then the years growing up in the boys' home in Lower Hutt and Sedgley in Masterton were now behind him. He was embarking on a new chapter in his life, and he wanted to make a completely new start. He wanted to leave behind all that had gone before. He wanted a new identity. Williams was the family name he had been born with, but in truth he had never really been a part of the Williams family. Indeed, the memory of his biological family was one of abandonment—first by his father and then by his mother—which had left him growing up and fending for himself in an institutional setting. David wanted to be done with that part of his life, and the best way to do it, he decided, was to change his name. Instead of being known as David Thomas Williams, he would change his name to David Thomas Bussau. Once he got to Timaru, he would make the change official by deed poll (a legal document drawn up to change a person's name). Besides, he reasoned, the name change would make it easier for him to fit in as a part of the Bussau family.

As the bus approached Timaru, David felt excitement rising. He was entering a new chapter in his life. Who knew what adventures lay ahead for him?

Chapter 5

A Budding Businessman

When the bus finally arrived in Timaru, Vera and Lyndsay Bussau, accompanied by Rocky, were waiting for David. Rocky ran to David and gave him a big hug as he stepped off the bus.

"It's so good to see you again," David said as he returned Rocky's hug.

They all drove to a rented house near the center of town, where Vera showed David to his room. It took David only a couple of minutes to unpack. He had left almost everything from his former life behind, and he looked forward to the fresh start that living in Timaru would offer him.

The next day David set out to explore the new place he now called home. Timaru was located about one hundred miles south of Christchurch, New

Zealand's third largest city. The town was nestled beside the sea on the edge of a large, fertile coastal plain. On a clear day, beyond the plain, you could see the majestic Southern Alps, sheer and snow-covered as they reached toward the heavens. Unlike Masterton, Timaru was a place where people came to vacation and be by the sea. Just a short distance from the heart of town was Caroline Bay, to which people flocked on sunny afternoons to stroll along the boardwalk and paddle in the chilly water of the Pacific Ocean. As David walked along the boardwalk that day, he decided that he was going to like living in Timaru.

By the time David finally arrived in Timaru, the new school year had begun. Although he had tried hard at Wairarapa College in Masterton, David had fallen short of passing his School Certificate, the national examination most New Zealand students took during their third year of high school. Once he had settled into life in Timaru, David enrolled at Timaru Boys' High School, where he planned to try again to pass his School Certificate. He also was eager to begin playing on the school sports teams. In addition, he joined a local soccer club and began regularly playing soccer.

After school David divided his time at home between playing with seven-year-old Rocky and doing chores around the house. It wasn't long, however, before he began to notice that his relationship with Vera and Lyndsay Bussau was different than it had been at Sedgley. As time passed, instead of feeling a part of the family, he began to feel like the house slave. Lyndsay and Vera were always having him do things around the house: mow the lawn, weed the garden, wash the dishes, dust the furniture—and the list went on and on. But David willingly and without complaint did whatever they asked of him, if for no other reason than he had no one to complain to.

Back at Sedgley, David had noticed that Vera could get quite angry at times, yelling at her husband at the top of her lungs. In Timaru her outbursts in the house were even more volatile and frequent. Much to David's disappointment, family life with the Bussaus reminded him of the grim days with his own family in Moera before being sent to boys' home. Gone was the fantasy of the cozy, warm family relationship he had daydreamed about before coming to Timaru. David realized that the only one who seemed to care about him as a person was Rocky. In fact, David began to wonder whether all that Lyndsay and Vera Bussau really cared about was his labor and getting their hands on the two thousand pounds he had received as a result of the injury to his hand. The money was still being held in trust for him until he was eighteen years old.

To make matters worse, things were not working out at high school. Although he enjoyed playing on various sports teams at Timaru Boys' High School, as in Masterton, David couldn't seem to muster the discipline necessary to apply himself in the classroom. Finally, after six months of trying, he decided it was time for him to leave high school and get a job.

David explained his predicament to his soccer coach, who worked at the local telephone exchange during the day.

"How would you like to work at the exchange?" the coach asked.

"I think that would be all right," David replied, unsure as to what a job in a telephone exchange might entail.

"I'll see what I can do for you," the coach said.

A week later David was working at the local telephone exchange in Timaru. But even after trying as hard as he could, he could find nothing to like about the job. After two months David quit and went to work at Hendersons, a local sports store. This was a job he liked, selling and repairing various kinds of sports equipment. Before long he was repairing fishing rods and reels, fixing cricket bats, restringing tennis racquets, and cleaning and reconditioning shotguns and hunting rifles.

At Hendersons David worked alongside Don, an Olympic champion cross-country skier from Canada who had come south to New Zealand to train during the northern summer. Don was several years older than David, but the two of them struck up a friendship. Often David would tag along with Don on the weekends as he headed for the Southern Alps to go skiing, a new sport to David but one he seemed to have a natural ability for.

Don also introduced David to another new adventure—flying. Don had a private pilot license, and on several occasions he rented a Tiger Moth biplane at the local airport and took David flying with him. David didn't quite know what to expect the first time he climbed into the open cockpit in front of Don. The Tiger Moth bounced down the runway before lurching into the air, and David gripped the sides of the cockpit until his knuckles turned white. But once they were airborne, he began to relax as Don guided the aircraft higher and circled out over the Canterbury plain. The view was magnificent. Off the right wing were the Southern Alps, and off the left wing was the dark blue Pacific Ocean. When he looked down, David could see the patchwork of fields spread across the plain below. As they flew, the wind rustled through David's hair and buffeted his face. All in all, David thought flying was an exhilarating experience.

During their working hours at Hendersons, David and Don had an ongoing competition. They would take turns serving the girls who came into the store and see who was the first to get a date with one of them. David had to admit that in this competition Don always had the better of him. Since Don was older and had a Canadian accent, the girls were more interested in going out with him than with David.

At the same time that he began working at Hendersons, David moved out of the Bussau house and into a small flat. He still visited the Bussaus regularly and spent time with Rocky, who had grown very attached to him. But living alone in a flat gave David some space and a lot more free time, which he soon found a way to fill up.

Early one evening as David strolled along the boardwalk at Caroline Bay, he stopped beside a hamburger stand and watched as customers lined up. The line was long, and he wondered whether the owner of the stand might need some help serving customers. During a lull in the line, he went up and spoke to the Greek owner of the hamburger stand. Sure enough, the owner was eager for some help, and David began working at the stand during the weekends. Before long, he was also working there in the evenings after he got off work at Hendersons.

Serving hamburgers was not too much different from serving hot dogs, as he had done back in Masterton, and David quickly mastered the job. As he worked, he thought about his experience with the hot dog stands back in Masterton. Perhaps, he thought, he might be able to duplicate that success with a hamburger stand.

"Would you be willing to sell your business to me?" David asked the owner one evening.

"I could be," the owner replied in his thick Greek accent.

After some negotiation it was agreed that David would purchase the business for one thousand pounds, which he would pay off in installments. The two men shook hands, and David found himself the owner of a hamburger stand set up in a trailer at Caroline Bay in Timaru.

Now that he was the owner, David got busy working long hours developing the business and making it more profitable. For nearly a year he labored away until he felt he had built a solid and profitable business, and then he sold his hamburger stand for a healthy profit. With the money he made from the sale, David invested in another business, a fish-and-chips stand located farther along Caroline Bay.

Again David saw the potential in this business and set to work maximizing that potential. Before long, his new business had twice the turnover it had when he first bought it. But while David enjoyed the challenge of building up a business, once the business reached the goals he'd set for it, he began to lose interest and look for a new challenge. That was what happened with the fish-and-chips business. Now that it was operating well and making a good profit, the day-to-day managing of the business began to bore David, who then decided it was time to sell. Again David made a good profit from the sale of the business and began to look around for a new challenge. His friend Don had recently left Timaru to return to Canada, and David decided that his next challenge also lay elsewhere, away from Timaru, in Auckland.

Located in the northern half of North Island on an isthmus between the Pacific Ocean and the Tasman Sea, Auckland was New Zealand's largest city. David had never been there before and decided he would like to see what opportunities it had to offer.

Rocky was heartbroken when David told her he was leaving Timaru. He understood how she felt. Over the years he had grown fond of her and would miss her. Still, he promised to write to her often and visit her whenever he could.

His farewell with Rocky over, David left Timaru behind and headed north to Auckland, carrying with him the five thousand pounds he had netted from selling his fish-and-chips business plus the compensation for his injured hand.

Nineteen-year-old David Bussau arrived in Auckland in early 1960 after spending nearly two years in Timaru. As he walked down Queen Street in the heart of Auckland for the first time, he was surprised at how big and bustling the city was. Queen Street ran all the way down to the edge of the harbor. When he reached the end of the street, David caught a glimpse of the big, new harbor bridge that had been opened the year before. The bridge was bigger than any bridge he had ever seen. The city seemed to exude an air of confidence, and David, too, was confident that Auckland was going to be a good place for him. Of course, he first had to find a place to live and a job.

David rented a room in a boarding house in Manurewa, one of Auckland's southern suburbs, and then found a job in a fertilizer factory nearby. It wasn't the greatest of jobs, bagging and labeling fertilizer, but David didn't mind the work. To supplement his income, he drew on a skill he had learned while working at Hendersons in Timaru. In the evenings and on weekends he busied himself restringing tennis racquets. It was a lonely existence, as David had no friends in Auckland, but he was certain that given time, the situation would eventually rectify itself.

After several months of living in Manurewa, David decided he wanted to live in one of Auckland's inner-city suburbs. He began scouring the newspaper and eventually came across a small advertisement that read, "Lodgers wanted: Family home, all meals provided, and washing done. Three pounds per week." The house was in Sandringham, and it seemed to David to be just what he was looking for.

The next day David knocked on the door of the house. A young woman opened the door. "Hello," David began. "I'm David Bussau, and I've come about the room you have to rent."

The woman introduced herself as Betty Jamieson and proceeded to tell David that she and her husband, Ron, had decided to take in three boarders to bring in a little extra income for the family. If David was prepared to share a room with one of the other boarders, he was welcome to move in. David accepted the offer, and by the end of the week he was living in the Jamieson house in Sandringham. It was a cozy fit. The house had only three bedrooms, and besides having three boarders, the Jamiesons had three children, who slept in the living room while a basement bedroom was being finished for them.

Despite the tight squeeze in the house, David enjoyed living with the Jamiesons. He got along well with Ron Jamieson, who, oddly enough, was also missing a finger. The two men also shared a love of soccer. David and Ron spent their Saturdays watching local soccer matches and working on projects around the house. David also liked spending time with Betty Jamieson. Betty was warm and outgoing, and David admired the way she handled her children. He wished his own mother had been a bit more like her.

Soon after arriving to live with the Jamiesons, David began looking around for another business in which to invest. He settled on the Busy Bee Bakery. The business was located in Newmarket, a suburb close to downtown Auckland. Newmarket was a mixture of office buildings and light industrial plants, a short commute from David's new home in Sandringham. What was even better, the bakery had potential for growth and the current owner was eager to sell it. This meant that the owner was willing to let David make a down payment on the business and pay off the remaining balance in installments. The owner also offered to stay for the first month and show David all he needed to know to run the bakery successfully.

Once again David was working in the food industry. He had successfully learned how to manage and run a hamburger business in Timaru before doing the same with a fish-and-chips business. He did not think it would be too much of a stretch to run a bakery, but he soon discovered that it was a lot harder than he had anticipated. During the first month at the bakery, David huddled in the back with the owner while a salesgirl served customers in the front of the store. The owner showed David how to knead dough and make bread and how to bake sponge cakes, meringues, pavlovas, pies, and buns. He made it all look easy, but after the month was up and he had left the bakery entirely in David's hands, things were not so easy for David.

Every item sold in the Busy Bee Bakery was baked fresh on the premises each day. David rose early each morning so that he could be at the bakery to start work at 4:00 AM. By eight o'clock one Tuesday morning, shortly after he had taken over running the bakery, David had baked the bread and buns for the day and after two attempts had finally produced a batch of passable sponge cakes. Now he turned his attention to producing a dozen pavlovas—large, round, fluffy meringue-like cakes that New Zealanders slathered with fresh whipped cream and fruit and ate for dessert. He separated the whites of three dozen eggs and placed them in the bowl of the commercial mixer, added the other ingredients, and set the machine to mixing. When the machine had beaten the egg-white mixture to a stiff foam, David made twelve piles from the foam, place them on two large trays, and slid the trays into the oven.

When he came to take the trays out of the oven an hour later, David couldn't believe his eyes. Instead of seeing twelve fluffy pavlovas on the trays, all he saw were twelve sticky egg-white pancakes. What had gone wrong? David had meticulously followed every step of the recipe. He dumped the two trays onto the counter and collapsed onto a sack of flour. Tears of frustration ran down his cheeks, and David began to have doubts about this new venture. Had he made the right decision by buying the bakery? Why was he having so much trouble with the baking? If he didn't get the baking right, he risked losing the business and all the money he had invested in it. He felt exhausted and very alone.

Despite his frustration, David knew he had to keep going. He knew that the problem had a solution, and he would just keep searching until he found it. The solution to his baking woes came in two ways. First, David simply refused to give in to the temptation to give up. When some item he was baking did not turn out right, he set it aside and started over, trying to analyze what the problem might have been and adjusting for it. The second thing he did was talk to the sales representatives who came to the bakery to sell him the various dry goods used in the baking process. Not only did many of these representatives have experience in the baking industry, but also they regularly visited other bakeries and observed how things were done there. David found them more than willing to answer his questions and offer advice. Before long their advice and his hard work paid off. Soon David was pulling perfect sponge cakes and pavlovas from the oven each time.

Once he had mastered the art of baking, David began to diversify the business. He began making and selling sandwiches, and he branched out into some catering. The Newmarket School for the Deaf was located across the street from the Busy Bee Bakery, and David started by catering for various events there. Before long he was also catering for business and professional lunches throughout the area. Of course, all this extra business began to create a nice profit in the day-to-day operations of the bakery, and David could not have been happier.

By early 1962 David had been in Auckland for two years. The Busy Bee Bakery was thriving, and he was still enjoying living with the Jamiesons. Yet David was still missing something—friends his own age. Finally he decided to do something about it. He planned to go to St. Chad's, the local Anglican church, the next Sunday and check out the youth group there.

Chapter 6

Someone Special

St. Chad's Anglican Church was the first church David had attended since leaving Sedgley Boys' Home in Masterton. Yet as he walked into the place for the first time, he felt at home. And to his delight, the church youth group was holding a planning meeting to discuss the upcoming year's activities. Excited to be among a group of young people, twenty-two-year-old David jumped right in, making all sorts of suggestions about possible group activities.

As the discussion progressed, David particularly noticed one of the girls in the meeting. The girl was tall and slender, with grey eyes and short-cropped brown hair. What he liked most about her was the broad, open smile that spread across her face as she whispered to the girl sitting next to her. He would have liked to have gotten to learn a little more about

73

her, but despite his brashness in offering the group ideas for possible activities, David was too shy to introduce himself to the girl and ask her some questions.

Still, David liked the experience of the planning meeting, and soon he was regularly attending church youth group meetings. About thirty young people came to the group, and they were a lively and interesting bunch. Sometimes the group went on outings together to the movies or to a dance. From time to time they held weekend retreats on Waiheke Island, an hour's boat ride away in the mouth of Auckland's harbor.

During the week David continued to put in long hours at the Busy Bee Bakery. His hard work there had paid off, and the business was booming. Some nights he was so tired at the end of a long day of work that he never made it back to his room at the Jamieson house. Instead he would slump down on a pile of flour sacks and sleep the night right there. But with all this hard work, David now had something to look forward to at the end of each week—youth group.

As he regularly attended St. Chad's youth group, David got to know the other young people who came, among them the girl he had noticed at the first meeting. The girl was eighteen years old and an only child, and her name was Carol Crowder. She played piano and sang in the church choir. Carol was in her second year at Epsom Teachers' College, where she was training to become an elementary school teacher. The more David talked to Carol, the more he liked her. Carol seemed conscientious and sincere and had a way of accepting other people as they were, a trait that David also possessed.

David was aware that he wasn't the only person interested in Carol. Several other young men in the youth group also fancied her. Undeterred, David plunged on ahead getting to know Carol better. He learned that her father was the manager of the shoe production division of Farmer's, a large department store in the heart of downtown Auckland. As a result of his position, Carol's father had been able to get Carol and her best friend, Sherryl, a job working at the department store on Friday evenings when it stayed open until nine o'clock.

Finally, after several months of attending the youth group, David mustered up the courage to ask Carol out on a date. To his surprise, she accepted. Several nights later David picked Carol up in his blue Bedford van from the bakery and escorted her to the local cinema to see a movie. David enjoyed the experience, and he guessed that Carol must have as well, because soon they were going out together regularly. But they experienced some bumps along the way. On two occasions David failed to show up for scheduled dates. Exhausted from his day's work at the bakery, he had gotten on his perch atop the flour sacks to rest for a short while before going to pick Carol up and failed to wake up. However frustrated Carol may have been about his failure to pick her up, she was gracious about the slipups and continued to go out with David, much to his relief and delight.

Another outcome of David's involvement with the youth group was that after attending the group for about a year, he moved out of the Jamieson house and into a two-bedroom flat in Mt. Albert, a neighboring suburb of Sandringham. Two other young men from the youth group lived at the flat, and David shared a bedroom with one of them, Bruce Fuller. David enjoyed the new living arrangement. The boys would sit around for hours and talk about all sorts of things, though talk about girls and dating was never far from their minds. The flat was a place where people liked to gather. It wasn't uncommon for David to come home from his day at the bakery and find it bursting at the seams with young people.

As David and Carol spent more time together, Carol began to open up to him about herself and her struggle with a nagging sickness. She explained to David that when she was fourteen years old, she had blacked out and collapsed while returning home from attending the Auckland Easter show with her parents. After a number of tests, the doctor diagnosed her condition as epilepsy and put her on heavy doses of medication to control the illness. Despite the medication, Carol continued to have seizures. She explained to David how embarrassed she was by the condition and that only a handful of people at church knew about it and covered for her if she had to leave an event early because of a seizure.

David listened attentively as Carol talked, though he didn't understand much about epilepsy and how debilitating it could be. Despite the condition, as time went on, David found himself falling deeply in love with Carol, and he began spending more time with her.

David still kept in contact with the Bussaus, mostly through regular correspondence with Rocky. The Bussaus had moved from Timaru to Raglan, a beachside community about one hundred miles south of Auckland. Now that he was in love and had a steady girlfriend, David decided that he would like to take Carol to meet the Bussaus, as they represented the only thing that resembled parents and family in his life.

Early on a Saturday morning, David and Carol climbed into the bakery van and headed south from Auckland. The drive through the rolling green New Zealand countryside was beautiful, and the trip was made all the better for David by having Carol at his side. Three hours after setting out, they drove into Raglan and found the Bussaus' house. When they pulled the van into the driveway, Rocky bolted out the front door to greet them. She gave first David and then Carol an enthusiastic hug, and she talked so fast that David could hardly keep up with her. Although Rocky's welcome was enthusiastic, Vera and Lyndsay Bussau's welcome was tepid at best. David introduced Carol to them, but they did not seem at all interested in her, and talk between the four of them was strained.

After several hours in Raglan, David and Carol set out on the drive back to Auckland. As they drove, a deep sense of disappointment and frustration overcame David. More than anything he had wanted Vera and Lyndsay Bussau to like and accept Carol. He wanted them to see all the wonderful qualities that he saw in her. And he wanted to embrace their acceptance of her as an affirmation that he had chosen well. But none of that had happened. Vera and Lyndsay had all but ignored Carol. It was a bitter blow that left David feeling very much alone.

David soon got over the disappointment he felt about the uneasy visit to Raglan. He kept busy at the bakery, and in the evenings he liked to visit Carol at her house.

One Friday evening, David was to escort Carol to a ball. He arrived back at his flat from his day at the bakery, exhausted as usual, and flopped onto his bed to rest a few minutes before getting ready. At seven-thirty the phone awakened him from his sleep.

"David, where are you? It's half past seven!" came Carol's voice on the other end of the line.

"I'm so sorry," David apologized. "I fell asleep. I'll be over in a half hour to pick you up."

David hung up the phone and sat groggily on the edge of the bed trying to shake off his sleepiness. But it didn't work, and he promptly fell back to sleep. He awoke with a start half an hour later, still not dressed and ready to take Carol to the ball. He picked up the phone and called her to apologize for not picking her up yet and to tell her that he would be there in twenty minutes. This time when he hung up the phone, David resisted the urge to nod off to sleep again. He showered and got dressed in his suit, but when he looked at the clock it was already past the twenty minutes when he said he would be there to pick up Carol.

Once again David telephoned Carol and explained that he would be over to pick her up in just a few minutes. He could tell from the dejected tone of Carol's voice on the other end of the line that she didn't believe him.

David finished getting ready, jumped into his Bedford van, and sped off to pick up Carol. As late as he was, he made one stop on the way to buy some pink roses for Carol. Two hours late, David finally knocked on the Crowders' door. When Carol opened the door, David was stunned at how beautiful she looked dressed in a flowing silk gown. He handed her the roses and apologized again for being so late.

Carol accepted David's apology and the roses, but on the drive to the ball she confessed that she wondered whether David loved business more than he loved her. This was a rebuke that David took to heart. Maybe it was time to sell the bakery. In the time that he had owned the business, he'd built it up and expanded it to maximize potential. Now his time was spent working punishingly long hours to keep things running. He began to wonder whether it wasn't time to sell and, as he had done in Timaru when he sold the hot dog stand, invest the money he made in another business that he could build up.

Finally David decided that it was indeed time for a change. After owning the Busy Bee Bakery for nearly three years, he sold the business for thirty thousand pounds, six times what he had paid for it.

With the profit from the sale of the bakery, David began to look around for a new business to buy. Finally he found what he was looking for—Betta Pikelets and Pancakes. The business, located in the suburb of Onehunga, produced pancakes, crumpets, and pikelets—small pancakes that New Zealanders slathered with jam and fresh whipped cream for morning and afternoon tea. David could see a lot of potential for development.

Now instead of working the large oven at the Busy Bee Bakery, David was hunched over a ten-feet-long by three-feet-wide hot plate to cook his wares. He soon discovered that the work was painstaking. First he had to mix the pancake batter and pour it into a large bag. Then he took the bag and went along the hot plate, squeezing out dollops of batter onto it. After he had squeezed out the batter, he raced back to the other end of the hot plate and began to flip the pancakes and pikelets to cook the other side of them. When he had flipped them all, he once again raced back to the other end of the hot plate to remove the cooked items from the heat and arrange them on trays to cool. Once they had cooled, a number of the pancakes and pikelets were bagged for delivery to local supermarkets. The items not bagged were delivered loose to bakeries around the city to be sold alongside other baked goods.

It didn't take David long to realize that there had to be a way to speed up and streamline the cooking process. He thought about it for a while and then approached Dudley Crowder, Carol's uncle, who was an engineer. Together the two men designed and built a pikelet-making machine. The machine, which basically consisted of a large hopper into which the pancake batter was poured, worked flawlessly. The hopper moved along above the hot plate, depositing in a row the batter for six pikelets, and then moved on to the next row. Now all David had to do was follow along behind the hopper, flipping the pikelets. The hopper could be adjusted to deposit more batter on the hot plate for pancakes.

David was pleased with the new pikelet-making machine, and he patented the device. Before long he and Dudley were tinkering with their invention, trying to automate the cooking process even more. This time they made the hopper stationary, and instead a circular hot plate, onto which the hopper deposited the batter, rotated below it. But this time, instead of David having to come along and flip the pikelets by hand, when they were cooked on one side, an arm flipped them off the hot plate and onto another hot plate below to cook the other side. Now with minimal effort David could cook thousands of pikelets and pancakes at a time without running from one end of the room to the other. With so much output, he began to look around for more markets for his product.

David worked out an arrangement with Tip Top and Fielders, two of New Zealand's largest bakers, to package his pikelets and pancakes and sell them under the their brand names. Soon David was busier than ever producing pikelets and pancakes overnight, packaging them, and delivering them to supermarkets throughout the city. He soon found that he was as busy as he had been at the Busy Bee Bakery and just as exhausted. In fact, early one Wednesday morning his exhaustion caught up with him.

As David guided the Betta Pikelets and Pancakes van along a two-lane city street, headed for a local Four Square supermarket to make a delivery, his eyelids began to close. He tried to fight off the extreme drowsiness, but he just couldn't do it. Moments later he was asleep at the wheel. Suddenly the van bounced up and then came to a stop with a loud bang. David awoke with a start as fresh pancakes and pikelets piled forward from the racks in the back of the van and landed on top of him in the driver's seat. He looked around and saw that the van had jumped the curb and careened into the center of a roundabout, coming to a stop when it collided head-on with a power pole in the middle of the roundabout. Miraculously, David was unharmed.

David clambered out of the van to inspect the damage, which turned out to be mostly superficial. The van's grill and hood were dented, but the vehicle still ran and was drivable. However, things inside the van were not quite so good. Pancakes and pikelets were everywhere. Those that were bagged were easily rearranged back on the racks. But the loose ones that David was to deliver to local bakeries took more effort. David had to painstakingly flatten out each pancake or pikelet and restack it on the racks. Finally, an hour after crashing, he was able to continue with his delivery route, driving as fast as he could to make up for lost time while being diligent not to fall asleep again at the wheel. More than one baker gave David a strange look that morning as he delivered the disheveled piles of pancakes and pikelets.

Despite David's exhausting work schedule, his relationship with Carol continued to blossom and grow. Finally he became confident that Carol Crowder was the person he wanted to spend the rest of his life with. He decided to ask her to marry him, and the perfect opportunity to pop the question, he decided, would be on an upcoming weekend trip they were planning to Mt. Maunganui, a beach community on New Zealand's east coast about two hundred miles from Auckland.

It was February 22, 1964, and a bright sun shined overhead as David and Carol followed the track up the side of the extinct volcano that gave the beach its name. About halfway up the track, they stopped to take in the view. On their left the deep blue water of the Pacific Ocean rolled ashore in an endless cascade of white crested breakers, and to their right small boats dotted around on the sheltered water of Tauranga Harbor. David decided it was now or never. He opened his mouth and said to Carol, "I suppose we should get married or something." The words weren't quite as eloquent as he would have liked them to be, but nonetheless, he had asked the question. David noted that Carol seemed to be taken a little by surprise at his question, and it seemed like an eternity to him before she replied. Finally she said, "I'd love to."

David was elated, and it was almost as if his feet did not touch the ground as he and Carol made their way to the top of the mountain. At the top they talked some more about life together and arranging a wedding, and David agreed that as a matter of formality he would ask Carol's father, Norm Crowder, for permission to marry his daughter.

Three days later, back in Auckland, David strode into the Crowder house in Sandringham. Norm Crowder sat at the kitchen table sipping a drink. "Norm, I'd like to marry your daughter," David announced.

Norm set his glass on the kitchen table, stood up slowly, and looked David in the eye. "Not in your life," he said as he spun around and headed out the kitchen door and into the garden to tend his rhubarb plants.

This was not the response David had expected from Carol's father, and he stood with his mouth open.

Carol's mother, Phyllis, or Phyl, as everyone called her, came over and tried to soothe David. "Give him ten minutes," she said. "He'll be back. It's the way he deals with change."

Sure enough, ten minutes later Norm appeared again in the kitchen. "So what was that you said? You want to marry Carol. Do you really mean it?"

David nodded.

"Well, let me think about it," Norm added.

He didn't have to think long and soon gave his approval.

David and Carol were delighted, as was Carol's mom, and they began to turn their attention to planning a wedding.

David looked forward to being a married man. One thing he promised himself was that when he and Carol were married and had children, he would be the most loving and attentive father a child could possibly have.

Wedding preparations had not gone too far, however, when a dark cloud descended over David and Carol's relationship.

Chapter 7

Change of Location

"A nervous breakdown? Is that really what's wrong with you?" David asked Carol.

Carol nodded, tears streaming down her face. "That's what the doctor said."

David scrambled to think of anything he knew about nervous breakdowns, but nothing came to mind. He'd never known anyone who'd had one. But now he was faced with the fact that his fiancée was in crisis. Carol had told David about the strange experience she'd had at her part-time job at Farmer's Department Store the previous Friday evening. She had felt herself mysteriously pulled toward the top of the ten-story stairwell in the middle of the store and experienced an overwhelming desire to throw herself down the stairs and fly to the bottom. Although

87

she had resisted the powerful urge to do so, David could tell, as she recounted the incident to him, that it had shaken Carol's confidence to the core, so much so that several days later she went soundly to sleep and did not wake up for two days. When she did wake up, she was a different person—groggy, confused, and unable to cope with her regular life.

Carol's mother whisked Carol off to the doctor, who prescribed powerful medication to control her condition. The medication, however, made Carol sleepy, and soon she was asleep more often than she was awake.

David found this to be a confusing time. He and Carol should have been excited about their impending marriage, but instead they were dealing with a mental collapse that neither of them understood. David wrestled with his feelings. There was no guarantee that Carol would ever make a full recovery, yet he loved Carol, and he supported her as best he could, even as she deteriorated. Carol began to develop strange phobias and obsessions. She would become mesmerized by trains and had to fight the urge to lunge at them as they hurtled along the tracks. And for some reason the color red had an effect on her, and she would often pass out when she saw a red dress or a red bus. As a result, she could no longer drive or continue her teaching career or do any of the other regular things she enjoyed, like singing in the choir at St. Chad's or attending youth group. She explained to David that the only thing she could do to get away from the voices and confusing thoughts flooding her mind was to sleep. Sleep became a refuge from her distorted reality.

While David tried to do everything he could to comfort and support Carol, he kept busy with Betta Pancakes and Pikelets. The business was thriving, and he decided to turn the distribution network he had developed for his product into an independent company, which he sold off. He then divided the remainder of the company into three divisions: manufacturing, export, and administering the patent rights to the pikelet-making machine that he and Dudley Crowder had developed. Now instead of having to deliver his pancakes and pikelets to over fifty stores around Auckland each morning, he handed them off to the distribution company, which did the work for him. All David now had to do each morning was get the product he was exporting to Auckland International Airport so that it could be loaded onto the 6:00 AM flight to Noumea, the capital of the Pacific island nation of New Caledonia. By nine o'clock his pancakes and pikelets would be on the shelves of Noumea's supermarkets.

Slowly, over many months, Carol stabilized a little, and with the help of her mother Carol was able to begin making wedding arrangements. David, though, could see that it was not easy for Carol, who was still in a fragile psychological state. Also, the medication Carol took left her tired and disconnected from reality.

Finally the wedding date was set for May 8, 1965, and the invitations were printed and sent out. David made sure that an invitation was sent to Rocky and the Bussaus, the only people outside of his and Carol's mutual friends he knew to invite to the wedding.

With great effort, all the details for the wedding were finally arranged, and at lunchtime on Saturday, May 8, David pulled on the coat of the new black suit he had bought for the occasion, adjusted his bow tie one last time, and headed to St. Chad's to be married. As the church filled with the invited guests, David took his place at the altar. Moments later the organ burst to life with the strains of "Here Comes the Bride." David turned to see Carol enter the church on the arm of her father. To David she looked stunning, dressed in her white lace wedding gown and veil. David knew, however, how stressful this moment was for Carol with all eyes on her and that as a result she was heavily medicated for the occasion.

At the altar David took Carol's arm from Norm Crowder, and the vicar then led the couple in their marriage vows. Before David knew it, he was rolling back Carol's veil to kiss his new bride.

For David it was a near perfect day. He was now a married man. But the one disappointment was that the Bussaus had not come to the wedding.

Following the wedding, David and Carol set out for South Island for their honeymoon in the small van David had bought for the trip. They were both relieved to have the pressure of organizing a wedding behind them as they drove to Wellington and then crossed by ferry to Nelson on South Island. They then made their way to Christchurch, Queenstown, and Milford Sound, staying in hotels when they could and sleeping in the back of the van when there were no rooms to be had.

After returning to Auckland, David went back to work at Betta Pancakes and Pikelets, but Carol was still not well enough to return to her teaching career.

As they thought about their future together, one of the things David realized they would have to plan for was a place of their own in which to live. Soon after the wedding he bought several acres of wooded land in Titirangi, one of Auckland's western suburbs, where he intended to have a house built for him and Carol to live in.

The early months of David and Carol's life together was dominated mostly by Carol's continuing illness. The only course of action that her doctor could come up with was to keep her on a heavy dose of drugs. But the drugs made Carol tired and zombie-like. It was a frustrating situation for both her and David. Then one day, as David accompanied Carol to see the doctor, the doctor called David aside for a private conversation.

"Perhaps a complete change might be good for your wife's condition," the doctor suggested. "Perhaps being away from all the pressure that may have contributed to her breakdown would be good for her. Perhaps in a different location she would feel more relaxed—more herself."

The doctor's suggestion held a lot of *perhapses*, but David began to seriously consider the advice. Finally he decided to take the doctor's recommendation. He had an entirely new and different setting in mind for them both—Sydney, Australia.

David sold his Betta Pancakes and Pikelets business for a good price, allowing the new owner to make a down payment and then pay the business off in installments. He then booked passage on the *Oriental Queen* to Sydney. His plan was to get a job in Sydney and see whether indeed the change of location would help Carol's condition. If it did, they would eventually return to New Zealand and build the planned house on their land in Titirangi.

In January 1966, he and Carol made their way up the gangway and onto the *Oriental Queen*. They stood on deck and watched as the vessel made its way out of Auckland Harbor and the city skyline faded from view. The ship sailed up the east coast of North Island and rounded Cape Reinga, New Zealand's northernmost point, before setting out across the Tasman Sea, the fifteen-hundred-mile stretch of ocean separating Australia and New Zealand. Three days later the *Oriental Queen* docked in Sydney, and David and Carol checked into a hotel in the Kings Cross area of the city.

Sydney was a bustling city with the same population as New Zealand crammed within its boundaries. David set to work looking for a job. Within days of arriving in the city, David had purchased a bicycle and was getting up at four in the morning to deliver copies of the *Sydney Morning Herald* to various residences. He also worked as a laborer during the day, and in the evenings he returned to an old craft—restringing tennis racquets. At the beginning of the week he would collect the tennis racquets from sports stores around the city and return with them to the flat he and Carol rented in Rose Bay on the east side of the city. Then in the evenings he would restring them and return them to the sports stores at the end of the week. Some weeks he had up to fifty tennis racquets to restring, which kept him very busy.

Then one day as David scanned the edition of the *Sydney Morning Herald* he had delivered to homes that morning, he spotted an advertisement in the employment section of the paper that piqued his interest. A local construction firm wanted to hire a foreman, and David decided that he was the man for the job, despite the fact that he had little experience as a carpenter—and none as a foreman. Deep down he knew that given the chance, he could do the job. He was a quick learner, and he was good when it came to organizing and supervising other people.

The next morning David found himself shaking hands with Jack Ginnery, the owner of the company looking to hire a foreman. As the two men talked, something seemed to click between them. David sensed that beneath Jack's short, rugged exterior was an honest man that he could work with. Before he knew it, David had the job.

That afternoon David headed straight to the library, where he sat and read every book on construction that he could lay his hands on. By the time he showed up to start the new job, David knew, at least technically, as much about construction techniques as the men he was supervising. Once on the job, he learned even more by watching carefully as the men worked. Before long David was working alongside the others, wielding a hammer as if he had been a carpenter all his life. And there wasn't anything he was not willing to try his hand at. If new plumbing or electrical wiring needed to be installed, David was up for the task. He would work away, figuring out the problems as he encountered them and storing away the solutions to the problems to draw on the next time he did some plumbing or wiring.

As David worked away as foreman at the construction company, he and Jack developed a friendship that transcended the boss-employee relationship. When David confessed to Jack one day that the Anglican church that he and Carol had been attending since arriving in Sydney was dead boring, Jack responded, "Why don't you come along to the church I attend? It's pretty active. I think you might like it."

The following Sunday, David and Carol showed up at Waverly Methodist Mission in the Sydney suburb of Bondi Junction. From the moment they set foot inside the church door, they felt right at home, so much so that they soon became regular attenders at church services. David particularly enjoyed the deep sense of spirituality and the way the church was actively involved in the community. Before long he was driving a bus once a week, transporting elderly people from their homes to the church hall, where older folks, or evergreens, as the church called them, were given a meal and a night's entertainment. He and Carol also became involved in helping to run the youth group, and Carol felt strong enough to do some teaching in a kindergarten run at a sister church in nearby Paddington.

David was pleased by the turn of events. Not only had they found an active church to be involved in, but also the change of location had perked Carol up, though she continued to take medication to control her condition and struggled with the lethargic feeling it cast over her.

Several months after moving to Sydney from Auckland, David and Carol were out shopping in the Bondi Junction area. As they strolled along, they came upon a couple also out shopping. David could hardly believe it when he recognized them. It was Wocky and his wife, Diane. "I can't believe it. What are you doing here?" David asked.

"We moved here about six months ago," Wocky replied. "I got a job with the Australian government designing overseas embassies. What brings you here?"

David told him about coming to Sydney and finding a job as a foreman. Wocky was impressed that David had been able to do that, since David had no prior experience.

The two men had not seen each other since they had parted ways from Sedgley. They talked away, filling in each other on the details of their lives since that time. Wocky had gone on to university from Sedgley and earned a degree in engineering. He had also married Diane, whom he had started dating while still in

Masterton. And interestingly, Diane and Carol had the same birthday. The two couples agreed to keep in regular contact with each other now that they were living in Australia.

The on-the-job relationship between David and Jack continued to grow, and before long the two men were partners in the construction company. Several years before, an accountant had swindled Jack out of a lot of money, leaving his construction business teetering on the edge of bankruptcy. As a result, the company could take on only smaller construction jobs because suppliers would not extend credit to Jack, insisting that he pay cash for the supplies he bought from them. David, however, because of his good credit history, established a credit line for the business that allowed them to take on larger, more lucrative building contracts.

As much as he was enjoying working in construction, David also had a hankering to see more of the world. When he and Carol learned that Dale and Eric Nyback, whom they had befriended at church, were returning to their native Canada, they decided to travel with them. David and Carol decided that if they liked Canada, they might settle there, and to that end Carol applied for a teaching job in Prince Rupert, British Columbia.

In mid-1967, the two couples set sail from Sydney aboard the liner *Marconi* bound for Naples, Italy. The trip would take two weeks to complete via the Suez Canal, but when the ship reached the Suez Canal, fighting had broken out between Egypt and Israel, and the canal was closed to shipping. The ship was forced to spend the next month making its way around the tip of Africa and then up the Atlantic Ocean to the Mediterranean Sea to reach its destination.

The voyage was tedious for David. The extra four weeks it took to reach their destination was almost too much for him to bear. He tried his best to fill in the time, and he admired the way Carol could sit calmly on deck and while away the hours reading books. To help break the monotony, in the mornings he and Carol attended Italian lessons on board, and to David's surprise he had a natural ability for learning languages. By the time they reached Naples, David was able to make himself understood quite well in Italian to the locals.

The two couples bought a car together in Naples and set out to see Italy and then made their way across Europe. When they reached Amsterdam, the Nybacks flew on to Canada while David and Carol traveled on to England. When they reached London, the Bussaus realized that their finances were running low. David took a job working in a bread factory at night and on construction sites during the day while Carol worked in a chocolate factory hand-wrapping Easter eggs and other chocolate confections.

Finally, after earning some money in London, David and Carol made it to Vancouver, Canada, where the Nybacks lived. By now Carol had heard that the teaching job in Prince Rupert was hers if she wanted it, and they did some research on Prince Rupert to check the city out. Tucked just below Canada's border with Alaska, it was a cold and isolated place, and both David and Carol had doubts about whether it was the place for them.

David and Carol moved on, first to Japan and then to the Philippines. David had observed small pockets of poverty in some of the ports of call the *Marconi* had made on the way to Naples, but in Manila, the Philippines' sprawling, overcrowded capital, he saw firsthand poverty on a scale that he had never seen before. He wished that he could do something about it, but he was just one man passing through on a visit, and what difference could one man make anyway to such an overwhelming problem?

A year after setting out from Australia, David and Carol arrived back in Sydney, where they rented another flat in Rose Bay. David went back to working with Jack Ginnery at the construction company while Carol took a job at Dymocks, a large bookstore. It felt good to be back in Australia. The couple resumed regular attendance at Waverly Methodist Mission and were quickly absorbed in various church activities.

Carol worked at Dymocks for over a year before she told David that she felt strong enough to take on the challenge of teaching again. David encouraged and supported her as she took a job at Rose Bay Elementary School. The class she taught was challenging. The children were hard to control, and Carol fought hard to focus on their schoolwork. When Carol learned that the teacher she had replaced had left with a breakdown, she quipped to David one day, "The teacher I replaced left with a breakdown, and here I am recovering from one." David smiled, amazed at how his wife was handling the difficult teaching assignment.

During this time Carol struck up a friendship with Jack Ginnery's sister, Ruth Moss. Ruth and her husband Alf and daughter Elizabeth lived in an old turn-of-the-century home on Darley Road in Randwick, across from Centennial Park. During the weekends the park was a haven for Sydney's residents who flocked there to walk or ride their bikes along its trails, ride horses, feed the ducks bobbing about on the many ponds that dotted the park, or just wander across the vast areas of grassed parkland. The location was wonderful, and Carol loved going to the house to visit Ruth.

Soon after New Year 1969, David and Carol received some wonderful news. Carol was pregnant. David was elated at the thought of becoming a father, yet both he and Carol were concerned about the effects that the drugs Carol took might have on the child. Still, it was time to think about their future as a family. As they thought about it, David and Carol came to the conclusion that the future for them was in Australia, not in returning to New Zealand. In fact, they had not been back to New Zealand in over three years. They liked the life they had created for themselves in Sydney and so decided to stay.

David was not content to just keep on renting a flat to live in, especially not with their first child on the way. If Sydney was to be their home, he wanted to own his own house there. When Alf Moss announced to David and Carol during lunch at the Moss home one Sunday that the house two doors down was for sale, David was immediately interested. He gulped down the rest of his meal, and then he and Alf went off to see the place. It was an old, rambling, two-story house that needed a lot of repairs, but it sat right across from Centennial Park on a large block of land. When David finally returned with Alf to the Mosses' home several hours later, he had a broad grin on his face and announced to Carol that he had arranged to buy the house for twenty-six thousand dollars.

David had to take out three mortgages to purchase the property, but he had a plan to pay the loans back as fast as he could. Once he and Carol took possession of the huge house, they got to work painting and repairing damaged floorboards and walls. The house was so big that David divided it into three apartments. He and Carol would live in the front apartment, and he would rent out the other two apartments, using the money he received to pay off his mortgages.

Now that they had a place of their own in which to live, David looked forward to the birth of their first child. At the same time, he threw his energies into developing the construction business.

Chapter 8

Booming Business

With each passing month of her pregnancy, Carol grew more tired, and David found himself doing most of the domestic chores around the house. He didn't mind, though. He was happy to think that he would soon be a father, and since he ran the construction company from home, he could work the chores around his business activities.

Business was booming at Carness Constructions, the company David and Jack Ginnery co-owned. Sydney was undergoing a building boom, and builders were in high demand. David and Jack's company specialized in renovating expensive houses in the exclusive Double Bay and Vaucluse areas of Sydney, and its services were in high demand.

When Jack decided that it was time for him to retire, David bought out his share of the business.

Soon afterward he formed two more companies, Bussau Constructions and Crowder Constructions. David managed the three companies, and each company took on separate building contracts. David had set things up this way so that in case one of the companies got into financial difficulty and was forced into bankruptcy, that company would not drag the other two companies down with it. David also set up a separate joinery business at the back of his property on Darley Road. There, Ari Neves, a French joiner, kept busy making the stairs, doors, and window frames needed for the various renovation projects the three construction companies were undertaking.

Between his construction business and taking care of Carol, David was kept very busy, but he didn't mind. He liked to work hard, and besides, he would have a baby to support any day now. That day arrived on October 29, 1969, when Carol delivered a baby daughter, whom they named Natasha. At twenty-eight years of age, David Bussau was finally a father. He and Carol were delighted when they learned that Natasha was a normal, healthy baby and had not suffered any effects from the medications Carol was taking.

From the start, David enjoyed his role as a dad. He spent hours playing with and cooing over Natasha.

At Christmas, Norm and Phyl Crowder, Carol's parents, arrived in Sydney to visit their daughter and see their new granddaughter. David could see that his father-in-law was particularly proud of Natasha and played up the role of doting grandpa to the hilt.

After ten days in Sydney the Crowders headed back to New Zealand. Phyl would like to have stayed longer, but Norm felt the need to get back to his shoe factory.

Six months after the Crowders had visited, David and Carol received the news that Norm had died of a heart attack. As sad as they were at learning of his death, they were also glad that he'd had the opportunity to see his granddaughter.

Between his duties as a father, David kept busy with the construction business. Then in April 1971, he and Carol received more good news. Carol was pregnant once again. On December 24, 1971, Carol gave birth to their second child, another girl, whom they named Rachel. Now David was the proud father of two girls. He could not have been happier.

Having one child to look after had been a challenge for Carol. This was not because she wasn't a good mother—indeed David was deeply impressed with her mothering skills—but because of the nagging tiredness she felt as a result of the medication she took for her condition. With two small children to take care of, things now became unbearable for Carol. She would become so tired and desperate for a nap that she would lay out toys for the children to play with and collapse onto the sofa to sleep, hoping the girls would wake her if they needed her.

David was not happy about the situation. He was concerned about what could happen to the girls while Carol slept. They might find a way out of the house, choke on something, or burn themselves on the radiators that warmed the house during the winter. Carol wasn't happy about the situation either. She was taking five different prescription drugs three times a day. One day she decided that she'd had enough. That night she told David that she had decided to stop taking all of her medications. "Those girls are depending on me. I have to pull myself together. I have to get out of myself," she explained.

David listened patiently. What Carol was planning to do was risky. But then so was leaving the girls alone while she slept. David had no idea what kind of journey they had set themselves on, but he was committed to Carol. If she thought she should do it, he would stand behind her 100 percent.

Carol was ready, and before David knew it, she had flushed her prescription drugs down the toilet. Without the medication, her body went numb as David tried to comfort her and take care of the children. He could see that withdrawing from the drugs was taking a toll on his wife, but she was determined. Carol refused to even consider going back on the medication. That was a quality David so admired in her. Once she set her mind to something, she never looked back, never second-guessed her decision.

It took two weeks, but Carol was finally able to confess to David that she felt remarkably better without the medication in her system. She felt more alert than she had felt in years. She also had more energy and effortlessly gave up her nap times. David was delighted, but like Carol, he was vigilant in case any of the symptoms of her illness returned. But none did. There were no more seizures, no more phobias, no more obsessions. Without these things that had dominated her life for so long, David watched as Carol's confidence and sense of self-worth began to grow with each passing day. To him she seemed alive once again, as though she had been set free from a cell in which she'd been imprisoned for years.

On the business front, things were going better than ever. The three construction companies had more work than they could handle, and David had just opened another business—a retail store selling wallpaper, tile, and bathroom and kitchen fittings. It helped the new store's bottom line that the store also supplied the three construction companies.

The focus of the construction business also began to slowly shift from remodeling homes to restoring old homes around the city. These homes were owned by very wealthy owners who were willing to pay the high costs of the restorations. David's companies had one of the best reputations in all of Sydney for quality workmanship and for completing a job on time. Architects and potential clients sought David out to work on their projects. In fact, they wanted so badly for his companies to do the work that he no longer had to bid on the contracts. The customers were willing to pay whatever it cost to have his company do the work. It was a business owner's dream.

Yet as time went on, David found himself becoming frustrated. He now employed one hundred workers, and rather than going out to job sites to work with his men, he was stuck in his office managing the

operation. His days were an endless stream of telephone calls, client meetings, and paperwork. Before
long he found that all this work was beginning to
encroach on other areas of his life. It was getting
harder for him to find the time to go jogging in Centennial Park, as he loved to do, or play on the church
soccer team. It was also getting more difficult to keep
up his involvement in various church activities. But
most of all, work was encroaching on his time with
his children. He loved to get down on the floor with
the girls and play, as he had done with Rocky back
at Sedgley. He and the girls would get blankets and
drape them over the dining room chairs to make forts
or would wrestle each other in the front room. For
David these were wonderful times, the times that
he'd never had with his parents when he was a child.
He wanted the girls to grow up knowing that they
were surrounded by loving parents who cared for
them and watched out for them.

One evening in mid-1974, as David was bathing
the girls, the telephone rang. He answered the call,
and a voice on the other end of the line said, "Are
you the builder who has been doing the work on my
house?"

David recognized the voice immediately—it was
that of Kerry Packer, media magnate and Australia's
richest man. One of David's construction companies
had recently completed some renovations at Packer's
house in Bellevue Hill. "Yes, I'm the builder," David
replied.

"Well get over here as fast as you can," Packer
demanded. "I'm having a party tonight, and the latch

on the cocktail cabinet you installed isn't working properly. I want it fixed before the party starts."

David took a deep breath. Couldn't the man live with a nonfunctioning latch on his cocktail cabinet for one night? David didn't want to go. He was in the midst of spending time with his children. But what choice did he have? Kerry Packer still owed him a lot of money for the job. "All right. I'll be over as quickly as I can," David replied.

David drove to Packer's luxurious home and in just a few minutes had fixed the latch. Although the whole affair had not been a huge inconvenience to David, somehow it touched something deep within him. When he left Sedgley and a life of growing up in a boys' home behind him, David had determined that he would never again allow himself to be put in a situation where other people had power over him, where they could dictate when and where and how he would do things and then punish him if he failed to meet their expectations. But as David thought about the situation with Kerry Packer, he realized that Packer—along with everyone else who still owed him money for work his construction companies had done—had the power over him. If he wanted the money, he had very little choice but to meet their demands, even if that meant leaving the children at night to fix the latch on someone's cocktail cabinet. This realization only raised the level of frustration David was feeling over his construction business.

Soon after the incident with Kerry Packer, David sat in his office pondering the report in front of him. He knew the recommendations were right, but he just couldn't seem to find the enthusiasm to follow through on them. David had hired a business consultant to give him advice on the next move for his construction businesses. The consultant had laid out in his report a new formulation for the company, rolling the three separate companies into one single corporation and borrowing a million dollars to invest in new, bigger, and better equipment for the business. Such a move, the consultant pointed out, given David's reputation for doing excellent work, would take his business to the next level, making it one of the major players in construction in Sydney. "But what was the point?" David asked himself. Sure, the business would make more money, yet an expanded company would only make him busier and take him further away from the things in his life he was already struggling to keep up with. And if he borrowed a million dollars as suggested, not only clients but also the bank would have power over him as they sought to protect their investment.

Over the next several months, David began to give a lot of thought to what might be the next step for his life. Yes, his company did good work, but there had to be more than just doing good work for clients. In fact, as he thought about it, he realized that what he enjoyed more than running a successful construction company was getting out into the community and helping people, as he had recently done with the Methodist church in Paddington. The church could barely bring in the money to pay the pastor's salary. To help offset church finances, the members of the congregation ran a small market outside the church, renting stalls to people who wanted to sell handicrafts, used clothing, food, produce, and the like. Seeing the church's situation, David had approached the pastor and suggested expanding the market. The pastor had agreed, and David and Sjaak Embrecht, a Dutch fitter and turner who rented one of the flats at the back of David's house on Darley Road, got to work. Together they built a large veranda around the outside of the church to provide some shelter from the weather for those renting the stalls. Then they made two metal trolleys on which to stack the tables used for the stalls. Their work paid off. The market rapidly expanded, and soon they had to make more trolleys for the ever-increasing stack of tables that needed to be moved and set up to keep up with the demand to rent stalls. Now the church was making more money from renting stalls at the expanded market than it had ever dreamed possible.

That was what David liked to do most: find a problem and come up with a workable solution that benefited the greatest number of people. Instead, he was stuck running a company where he now realized that other people had power over him. Yes, his management skills were responsible for the success of the construction business. However, he felt trapped by that success, since he now spent most of his time stuck in an office doing the things he least liked about business.

Yes, the business had been lucrative for him, but David began to wonder just how much money a person needed. When was enough enough? Was letting others have power over him really a worthwhile trade-off, just so he could earn more money? By now he certainly had plenty of money. In fact, he had surpassed his goal. He'd told the other boys back at Sedgley as they fixed their bikes together and voiced their dreams for the future that he planned to be a millionaire by the time he was forty. He wasn't yet thirty-five, and he had already done that. Wasn't that enough? There had to be something different out there for him, something that wouldn't leave him feeling the way he felt right now.

On Christmas Day 1974, David was still wrestling with his feelings and his future as he rose early to begin preparations for the Christmas dinner that would be served later in the afternoon. At Christmas, David and Carol often opened their home to those who had nowhere else to go. Usually a good number of people, including several people who worked for David, showed up at the house for Christmas dinner. People began to arrive at the house at one in the afternoon, at which time David left the kitchen and swung into host mode, greeting people warmly and wishing them a "Merry Christmas" as they arrived. Before long a crowd of people were milling around the house and in the backyard, where tables were set up on which to serve the food. By midafternoon, platters piled with food were spread on the tables, and people began helping themselves to Christmas dinner.

Inside after dinner, David flicked on the radio to catch the latest news of the day. "Dramatic news out of Darwin," he heard the announcer say. "The entire city lies in ruins after being hit by Cyclone Tracy."

David stood riveted to the spot. The radio report went on to say that the cyclone had struck Darwin, located in Australia's Northern Territory, late on Christmas Eve, and that while details were still sketchy, it was believed many people had lost their lives and most of Darwin's buildings had been leveled.

Soon others at the house were gathered around the radio listening to the news reports. Then later, the first television pictures of the disaster flickered across the TV screen in the living room. The devastation looked even worse than the radio reporter had described. The city of forty-eight thousand inhabitants was indeed in ruins.

As he watched, a strange idea struck David. Why not take a team of men to Darwin to help out with the massive cleanup and rebuilding effort that would be necessary? After all, it was summer vacation time in Australia, and the construction business would be closed down for the month of January.

David talked about the idea with Carol and several of his employees who were at the house, and they all thought it would be a good thing to do. In the days following, David called more of his employees, and a call for volunteers went out from the Waverly Methodist Mission. David offered to pay the men's airfare to Darwin in return for their labor, and a local church in Darwin would find accommodations for them, such as they were. Before long a group of twenty men were in on the project. David was energized. Here was an opportunity to help people in desperate need. The frustration he had been feeling over his construction business had been replaced by an excitement for the challenge ahead.

Less than two weeks after Cyclone Tracy hit Darwin, the group was headed for the airport in Sydney. David was anxious to get to Darwin and get to work.

Chapter 9

Darwin

A s the airplane circled the city and made its approach to land, David peered out the window, dumbstruck at the devastation Cyclone Tracy had wrought on Darwin. The city was damaged far worse than he could have imagined, worse than the images of the disaster on television had revealed. Barely a house was left standing in the city's northern suburbs, and debris was scattered in all directions.

As he stepped off the plane at Darwin's battered airport, David felt like he was stepping into a sauna. It was the wet season and the hot season in Darwin, and the resulting humidity was so thick and heavy it clung to his skin. By the time he had walked across the tarmac, beads of sweat were running down David's face and back.

David and his team stayed at a nearby hostel run by the Uniting Church, which had miraculously survived the ravages of the cyclone fairly unscathed. After the team had made it to the hostel with their duffel bags and toolboxes, David sprang into action. He set out to survey the damage and come up with a plan to deploy the members of his team in the most effective way. He had seen the aftermath of the cyclone on television and from the air as they flew in, but now he was viewing it at close quarters. Most of the houses in Darwin were built atop steel or concrete pilings, with stairs leading up to the living area and the laundry situated under the house. Lots of steel and concrete pilings were sticking up everywhere, but few houses were left intact on top of them. David walked down street after street where the combined effects of Cyclone Tracy's wind and flying debris had leveled everything. Cars, appliances, furniture, and personal belongings were strewn everywhere among the rubble. By the time David arrived in Darwin, nearly thirty thousand of the city's forty-eight thousand inhabitants had been evacuated or had fled the place, and those who had stayed huddled for shelter under what remained of their homes.

Before long David had a plan, and soon the members of the team were spread out around Darwin, putting their carpentry skills to work. They focused much of their efforts on houses that had been damaged but not destroyed by the cyclone. Some of these homes needed their roofs repaired or holes in the walls patched, while others needed bathrooms and kitchens put back into functioning order. So much work needed to be done across Darwin that the efforts of twenty men seemed insignificant, but they were not insignificant to those the men helped. With tears in their eyes, grown men would thank the workers for their efforts in giving them back a place to live. As David made it back to the hostel each evening dirty and sweaty, the thought of those thank-yous spurred him on to try to help even more people the next day.

Finally, after three weeks in Darwin, it was time for the team to head back to Sydney. Exhausted yet exhilarated from the experience, David clambered back onto the airplane. He took a last look at the devastated city of Darwin as the plane took off. So much work still needed to be done. It was going to take a long time and a massive rebuilding effort before the city could finally put the disaster of Cyclone Tracy behind it.

David hadn't been back in Sydney long before he again began feeling frustrated. Once more he was renovating and restoring the houses of some of Sydney's most wealthy residents, while across the country in Darwin so many people no longer even had homes in which to live. He wished he could do more for these people. He got his opportunity three weeks after arriving back from Darwin when the phone rang one evening.

"Hi, David. This is Doug McKenzie," the voice on the other end of the line announced.

The Reverend Doug McKenzie was a minister in Darwin who had coordinated and helped the team's efforts while they were there.

"Doug, it's so nice to hear from you. How are things in Darwin?" David asked.

"You know there's still a lot to be done. The Uniting Church wants to be involved in the ongoing rebuilding effort. We want to bring in work teams from across Australia to help us, and we need someone to coordinate those teams." Doug paused for a moment before continuing. "Someone like you. David, would you be willing to move up here to Darwin for a while with your family and take on that role?"

David wanted to say yes immediately, but he knew that a decision like this would have to be talked over with Carol, since it affected her and the girls as much as it affected him. "Let me talk it over with Carol and get back to you."

"And why would we do this?" was Carol's initial reaction when David told her about Doug's phone call. But as the two of them talked more about it, Carol warmed to the idea of going to Darwin. They agreed that it would be a challenge. They would be kept busy, but it could also be a lot of fun and a great break from the pattern their lives had fallen into in Sydney. David called Doug back and told him that the family would come to Darwin as soon as he could take care of business matters.

David set to work organizing his construction businesses so that they would carry on without him around. By now he had come to the conclusion that he wanted to sell the businesses, and he had stopped accepting new contracts and concentrated on completing several large contracts that were already under way. When the projects were finished, he would put the companies up for sale. Meanwhile, Vic Henshaw, the manager of David's tile and bathroom store, and his wife agreed to move into the Darley Road house and collect the rent from the flats at the back while David and Carol were in Darwin.

As soon as things were organized, David headed to Darwin. Two months later Carol and the girls joined him there. They lived in Gordon Symonds Hostel near the airport, where David and his team had stayed during their earlier trip to Darwin. Before Cyclone Tracy, the hostel had been a place for Aborigines to stay when visiting Darwin from outlying areas around the Northern Territory. Although visiting Aborigines continued to use the place, the hostel also served as home for the teams of workers coming from all over Australia to help with the reconstruction effort.

When Carol arrived, she took over managing the facility while David kept busy coordinating and managing the teams. And David had plenty to keep him busy. He was in charge of ordering the necessary building supplies so they would be on hand when teams arrived, and he also assigned workers to various projects. The teams of workers rebuilt church buildings, community buildings, and private homes in and around Darwin. Basically, David's teams were willing to undertake any job that would help the people of the city get back on their feet.

Besides purchasing new building materials for the jobs, David recycled as much as he possibly could. He would sift through piles of debris from the cyclone. "This is good. We can reuse this," he would say, and some of the men would set the item aside. Soon David had amassed a large pile of window frames, doors and door frames, and sheets of corrugated roofing iron that could all be used in the rebuilding effort.

While he and Carol were kept busy with their respective responsibilities, David always found time to spend with five-year-old Natasha and three-year-old Rachel. At the rear of the hostel was a trampoline, and soon David had the girls doing somersaults and backflips on it. After a heavy downpour of rain, he would take the girls swimming in large, rain-filled potholes around the hostel.

David also spent a lot of time away from Darwin, fulfilling the other responsibility of his job—recruiting teams of skilled workers to come to the devastated city. He would fly to various cities around Australia where he spoke in churches, describing the need for both workers and money for the rebuilding work in Darwin. At first this was not easy for him. He was a naturally shy person, and standing in front of a church full of people was nerve-wracking. But as David spoke at more and more churches, his confidence as a public speaker grew. Soon he no longer experienced the nauseating knot in his stomach as he waited to speak. And the words he had stumbled over at first now seemed to flow easily from his mouth.

After he had spoken, plenty of people were always willing to volunteer for the rebuilding task in Darwin. However, David would not allow just anyone to go to Darwin. Because he wanted skilled workers—carpenters, plumbers, electricians, and the like—after he had spoken at a church, he would spend time interviewing the volunteers to make sure they did indeed have the skills they said they had. Many people, he discovered, were eager to get to Darwin and see firsthand the damage Cyclone Tracy had meted out to the city. But the Australian government tightly controlled access to the devastated city, issuing permits to travel there only to skilled workers. As a result, people often told David they had skills that weren't up to the task. But David found that a few minutes of talking with each volunteer quickly sorted out the skilled tradesmen from the not-so-skilled or unskilled volunteers.

While he was away on his speaking and recruiting trips, David would travel to Sydney to see how things were going with his construction businesses. When all the outstanding contracts the companies had been undertaking were finally completed, he began the process of selling the companies.

Back in Darwin the rebuilding effort kept moving forward. A steady flow of teams came to the city, and with each passing month, Darwin began to emerge from the devastation of Cyclone Tracy. People started to return home to live, though many who had fled in the wake of the cyclone never returned. And many of those who had come to help in the various rebuilding efforts decided to stay. More and more, Darwin once again was beginning to look and feel like a city.

Finally, one day in late 1976, David arrived back at the hostel and said to Carol, "I think our time here is reaching its natural end. Fewer volunteer workers are coming, and the reconstruction money is drying up."

"You're right," Carol said, "So what do we do now?"

It was a good question. David did not want to return to Sydney, especially now that he was selling his construction businesses. Somehow, even though things were winding down in Darwin, he felt that he was at the start of something new—that there was more out there somewhere for him to do. And he knew that Carol felt that way too. All they had to do now was find out what that next thing was.

That next thing came as a result of an earthquake that occurred July 14, 1976, beneath the Indian Ocean. Seismic waves had radiated out from the earthquake and had wrought devastation on the nearby island of Bali, Indonesia. It had taken some time for all the damage to be assessed, especially in the isolated out-lying villages. Finally a request for help from Bishop Wayan Mastra in Bali had reached the Reverend Doug McKenzie in Darwin. Bishop Wayan Mastra wanted to know whether Doug knew of a good carpenter who could come to Bali and help rebuild a church in the isolated Christian village of Blimbingsari on the western side of the island that had been toppled by the earthquake.

"David," Doug said to David one day late in 1976, "my friend Bishop Wayan Mastra in Bali needs a skilled carpenter to come and help rebuild a church in a village destroyed by the earthquake. I immediately thought of you."

Without a pause David responded, "Yes, we'll go there."

Three weeks later, after being in Darwin for eighteen months, David and Carol and their two daughters were on their way to Bali.

Chapter 10

Blimbingsari

As the airplane winged its way west from Dar-win, David thought about the decision he had made to come to Bali, and the enormity of it hit him. He was taking his family to live in a remote Balinese village where they would be exposed to danger, disease, and strange cultural ways. The family would also have to support themselves financially throughout their time there. Since little money was available for the rebuilding project, David knew that he would have to use some of his own money to help the project along. Despite these drawbacks, he felt an excitement about what lay ahead. It was the next step for him and Carol—a step of faith—and as he took the step, he was certain that a new path would open up for them both.

The welcome the Bussau family received upon their arrival at the Denpasar airport in Bali was less than enthusiastic. An Indonesian customs official poured the contents of their suitcases onto a large table and began rummaging through their belongings, pocketing for himself those items that seemed to take his fancy. Finally, with a grunt and a wave of his hand, he turned and walked away, leaving the girls shaken and David and Carol scrambling to stuff their belongings—which by now were spread across the table and floor—back into their suitcases. Once they left the customs hall and emerged into the arrival area, however, things were different. Wayan Mastra was waiting for them, and he warmly welcomed David and Carol and the girls to Bali.

Bishop Wayan Mastra was a gregarious, caring man, and David liked him immediately. During the several days the Bussaus spent in and around Denpasar, Bali's capital, before heading to the village of Blimbingsari, Wayan told David about himself, the history of Christianity on the island, and his vision for the future.

Bali was a deeply spiritual place, where the predominant religion was Hinduism, and Hindu temples dotted the landscape. Wayan had himself been born into a poor Hindu family. However, he had been fortunate enough to attend elementary and secondary school, where he excelled. He had then attended college on the island of Java, where he converted to Christianity. After receiving his undergraduate degree, Wayan earned a scholarship and traveled to the United States to study at the University of Dubuque in Iowa, graduating with a PhD in 1970. He returned to Bali after receiving his degree and eventually became the leader of the Protestant Christian Church in Bali. As leader of the church, Wayan strongly believed that it should have a distinct Balinese cultural flavor. He also believed that the Bali church should be self-sustaining and not dependent on Western churches for support. He had ideas about training church members in various skills so that they could get well-paying jobs in the tourist industry that was just beginning to blossom in Bali. David admired Wayan's farsighted vision.

The bishop explained that for many years the Dutch, when they were the colonial rulers of Indonesia, would not let missionaries into Bali, but finally they had relented, and in November 1931 the first twelve Christian converts were baptized. However, as more Balinese converted, tensions began to rise between Christians and Hindus. In 1939 it was decided that the Christians on the island should relocate to an area known as Alas Rangda (meaning "the place of the evil one") located on the western tip of Bali. Alas Rangda was one of the most desolate places in the whole of Bali. Still, Made Runga, leader of the Christians at the time, led a group of twenty-nine Christian families on a seventy-mile trek west from Denpasar to Alas Rangda. There, amid the overgrown swampy jungle infested with snakes and tigers, the group carved out for themselves a clearing and built a village in the shape of a cross. They changed the name of the place from Alas Rangda to Blimbingsari, and over the years the village had continued to grow.

A Western-style church in the heart of Blimbingsari served as the center for village life. But the July earthquake had destroyed the church, and village elders desperately needed a new church to replace it—and not just another Western-style church. Instead, they wanted a concrete church built in the Balinese architectural style that would last for a thousand years, like the great cathedrals in Europe. David had never built a church before. That was going to be challenge enough, let alone making sure the building would stand for a thousand years. At least if it didn't last that long, he wouldn't be around to know about it.

Several days after arriving in Bali, the Bussau family set out for Blimbingsari. They followed the road that led west from Denpasar to Gilimanuk at the very western tip of Bali. For a good part of the journey the road wound along the edge of the coast, past gleaming white-sand beaches drenched by the blue water of the Indian Ocean. When the road left the coast, it rolled along hillsides terraced in rice paddies, a new crop of rice plants lifting their heads above the embankment that held back the water they grew in. As the family drove along, David was impressed by the beauty of Bali. The land was certainly a lot different from Darwin.

When the travelers reached the town of Negara, their vehicle turned north onto another road that would take them the final eight miles of their trip to

Blimbingsari. David found it hard to think of it as a road. It was more of a pothole-ridden track hacked through the jungle that could be negotiated only in a four-wheel-drive vehicle or on foot. Finally the bone-jarring ride came to an end, and the driver pulled the vehicle to a halt in Blimbingsari.

The first thing David noticed as he climbed from the vehicle and stretched his legs was the sea of inquisitive faces that began to pour out of the surrounding houses and gather around the vehicle. Then a man stepped forward and introduced himself as Ketut Arka, the local minister at Blimbingsari. He welcomed David and Carol to the village and then showed them to a white stuccoed, thatched-roof house a set on a rise. "This is your home. I hope you will be comfortable," Ketut Arka said.

The place was certainly more than David had been expecting. He had wondered whether the family might not all be holed up together in some bamboo hut, but this was a solid house with two small bedrooms, a living area, and a kitchen. The floors were concrete polished to sheen, and at the back of the place was a bathroom that contained a *bak,* a large concrete tub filled with water. Ketut Arka explained that water from the bak was scooped out and used for washing. David decided that he and Carol and the girls would be quite comfortable in the house.

After settling into their new home, David went for a stroll around the village. The signs of damage from the earthquake were all around. The church and several other buildings still lay in ruins, while many of the houses had patched-up holes in their walls or roofs to make them habitable again.

The next day David got to work on the rebuilding task. About one thousand families were living in Blimbingsari. The village elders, under the leadership of Made Runga, allocated a hundred men a day to work with David. The men's first job was to clear away the crumbled remains of the old church. David set the men to work while he pored over the plans for the new church, trying to work out the details of how best to build such a concrete structure in the middle of the jungle. Three weeks into the project David came to the realization that there was no way they could build the new church without an adequate water supply. To mix the amount of concrete the plans called for, he would need thousands of gallons of water, far more water than the paltry village well could provide. The nearest adequate water supply was a river several miles away.

David talked the situation over with the village elders, and it was decided that the first thing to do was to build a dam in the mountains and pipe water from the river down to the village. Not only would this provide water to mix the concrete, but also, a steady water supply to the village would improve everyone's life.

Once a site was located, David set about designing a dam. The project was challenging, since David had never actually built a dam. Eventually, however, David came up with a design he thought would work. First the men built a tunnel through which to divert the flow of the river. Once the water had been diverted, they set to work building the dam. David supervised the men as they hauled generators through the jungle and up to the site to run their equipment. The men then began drilling anchor holes into the bedrock into which they put reinforced steel rods and cement to hold the dam in place. It was a long process, but with one hundred men a day working on the project, the job began to move along. David showed the men what to do and how to do it and left them to do the work, coming back each day to supervise progress.

While work progressed on the dam, David put another group of men to work in the village, digging the foundations for the new church, building the forms in which to pour the concrete, and cutting and tying together the reinforcing rods needed to strengthen the concrete columns that would rise from the foundations to support the walls and roof.

Few of the residents of Blimbingsari spoke any English, but before long David had learned to speak passable Indonesian so that he could communicate with the workers. His Indonesian language skills helped him when he made trips to the city of Surabaya on the neighboring island of Java to purchase building materials, though it took several trips before he mastered the art of striking a good deal. Often when the building materials he purchased arrived at Blimbingsari, David would discover that they were of an inferior quality to what he had paid for. The bags of cement would be half filled with sand, and the timber would be knotted and twisted. Eventually David learned to inspect everything he purchased to make sure it was up to the quality he was paying for, and then he'd watch as it was loaded onto the truck for delivery to Blimbingsari.

In Blimbingsari David was delighted to see the way Carol was finding her niche. It had taken her a little while to adjust to life in the village. Inquisitive faces would appear at the window as she home-schooled Natasha and Rachel. At first it was difficult for Carol to communicate with the people. But as she began to learn some Indonesian words, she became more confident to venture farther afield in the village and speak to people. Soon Carol and René Arka, the pastor's wife, had become good friends, often stopping at each other's house to drink tea and talk. Carol began holding ongoing English lessons for those residents of the village who wanted to learn the language.

The Bussaus' life in Blimbingsari was made easier by Ketut Wasiati, the twenty-year-old house girl Ketut Arka had selected for them. Ketut Wasiati cleaned house, did the laundry, and went early in the morning to the market in nearby Melaya to buy the food for preparing the family's meals. She also was good with the children. At first Carol did not want a house girl. She felt uncomfortable having someone in the house serving the family. But Ketut Arka insisted she stay, assuring Carol that the family would get used to her being around and that her presence would make their lives easier. Sure enough, Ketut Arka was right. Before long the family were calling Ketut Wasiati

"Ketut Was," and David was wondering how they would have coped without her.

Natasha and Rachel seemed to love their new home. Often David would see them wandering among the rice paddies, catching frogs and snakes, or hanging out with the other children in the village. In no time at all they were both speaking Indonesian as if they had spoken it all their lives.

In April 1977 a group of volunteers from a church in Newcastle, Australia, arrived in Blimbingsari to help out in the village for two weeks. As the visitors walked around, they noticed that the children had no place in the village to play. They talked with David about their observation, and before long they came up with a plan: they would build a playground for the children right in the center of Blimbingsari.

The team got to work and had soon created a wonderful playground, complete with swings and a slide and seesaw. David was impressed with their work, and once the playground was finished, they all sat back to watch the children of the village enjoy it. But no children came to the playground. David quickly learned that the children in the village were much too busy after school to go and play. They had work to do—gather wood for the fire, fetch water from the well, tend crops, and prepare meals. The children who benefited from the new playground were Natasha and Rachel, who got to enjoy it often.

David learned an important lesson from the episode with the playground. In working to help develop a community, it was essential first to talk to the locals and find out what they thought was best for them, rather than assume what was good for the community. Had he as an outsider taken the time to consult the residents of Blimbingsari, David would have learned that the children did not need a playground, that the children were kept busy most of the time when they were not in school, and that the notion of children gathering to play in a playground did not fit in with their culture.

Meanwhile, work on the dam was progressing, as were preparations at the church site. David also supervised the building of a new school and medical clinic in the village. While he was kept busy with all the construction projects, every two weeks David would make a trip to Denpasar. Because there was no telephone in or around Blimbingsari, he would go to Denpasar to use the phone to conduct business. He would make calls to Australia, or people in Australia who knew that they could call him in Denpasar at certain times would phone him. It was during one of these visits that David received an unexpected phone call from Sydney.

"Hello," David said, putting the receiver to his ear.

"Hi, David. This is Leigh Coleman," came the reply at the end of the line.

"Leigh, nice to hear from you. It's been a while."

Leigh was the son of the pastor of Waverly Methodist Mission in Sydney and had attended the church youth group when David had been helping to run it. He had long hair and a beard and loved motorbikes. He would often arrive at youth group meetings on his motorbike with a group of friends in tow. At the meeting, Leigh and his friends would be disruptive and rude and create quite a scene. Leigh had managed to transfer his love of motorbikes into a franchise business repairing and selling prestige motorcycles in Sydney, and David had remodeled the showroom for him. But about the same time that David left Sydney for Darwin, Leigh left Australia for India, where he had spent time listening to gurus, practicing transcendental meditation, and generally seeking enlightenment. David had often wondered how much of Leigh's behavior was simply Leigh rebelling against the fact that he was the son of a pastor. Now Leigh explained that he was back from India and at loose ends in Sydney. He had heard that David was in Bali doing some construction work and wondered whether he needed some help for a while.

"Yes. Why don't you come on up here and I'll put you to work," David replied.

Several weeks later Leigh arrived in Blimbingsari. David did a double take when he first saw him; Leigh looked so different. He had lost weight, shaved his beard, and cut his hair. He was eager to get to work doing whatever David needed him to do. David soon had Leigh at work supervising the building of the dam.

As construction of the dam neared completion, pipes had to be run several miles down to Blimbingsari. However, the path of the pipeline ran through two Hindu villages. The residents of these two villages regarded the Christians of Blimbingsari with great suspicion, and David had to encourage the leaders of Blimbingsari to negotiate with the leaders of the two villages. It was not easy for them at first, but as the leaders of the three villages talked to each other, a level of trust developed among them. Before long the leaders of Blimbingsari had come to an agreement with the other two villages. They would supply the two villages with water from the pipeline in return for the residents from the two villages not sabotaging the pipeline. Before long, water was flowing down the pipeline to Blimbingsari, and concrete was being mixed and poured into the forms for the foundation of the new church.

As work continued on the church, Ron and Meg Hewitt arrived from Sydney. Ron was a builder, and he and David had been friends at the Waverly Methodist Mission. The Hewitts had come to Blimbingsari so that Ron could help out with the building. David was delighted to have them around, and he and Ron would sit together in the evenings reminiscing about life back in Sydney.

One day Ron was working on a beam at the mezzanine level of the new church, about ten feet above the ground, while David was up higher on a scaffold. As he worked, David heard a thump below him, like the sound of a sack of sand being dropped. As he gazed down, he saw Ron lying on the concrete below. David clambered down from his perch on the scaffold and ran to Ron. Somehow Ron had fallen off the beam and hit his head hard on the concrete. He was unconscious and bleeding, but he was still breathing.

Pak Nyoman Yusef, foreman on the church construction site, immediately jumped onto his motorcycle
and headed for Melaya, saying that he would be back
shortly with a car to transport Ron to the hospital.
However, no one in the village owned a vehicle other
than a motorcycle.

David tried to keep his unconscious friend warm
and comfortable as they waited for the foreman to
arrive with transportation. Two hours passed before
Yusef finally arrived with a *bemo,* a local taxi that was
basically a small SUV with a canopy on the back cov-
ering two wooden seats for passengers. David and
Yusef carefully loaded Ron into the back of the taxi,
and then David and Ketut Suweria climbed in, and
they were off to the nearest hospital. David and Ketut
Suweria cradled Ron's head in their arms as they
bounced down the rugged road from Blimbingsari.

"Sorry, we can't take him here. The accident didn't
occur in this region," the stone-faced supervisor told
the men when they finally arrived at the hospital.

David could hardly believe what he was hearing.
"But he could die if he doesn't get to see a doctor
now," he protested.

The supervisor just stared coldly at him, and no
amount of reasoning would change his mind. There
was nothing to do but head toward Denpasar and
hope that the next hospital would treat Ron. As they
raced on, however, David began to have doubts as
to whether his friend would make it. By now a large
pool of crimson blood lay on the floor of the taxi, and
Ron's breathing was getting shallower as the minutes

ticked by. Before the taxi reached the next hospital, Ron died, his head cradled in David's arms.

David was devastated. His friend was dead, and now he would have to break the news to Ron's wife, Meg. But before heading back to Blimbingsari, they drove to Denpasar to leave Ron's body at the morgue there.

Meg Hewitt broke down, convulsed by deep sobs when she learned of her husband's death. David and Carol tried to comfort her as best they could, and the next day David escorted Meg to Denpasar, where they made arrangements to fly Ron's body back to Sydney. David then accompanied Meg on the flight to Australia.

When he finally arrived back in Blimbingsari from Australia, David was still trying to make sense of Ron's death. Things weren't supposed to have worked out this way! Still, while in Australia David learned that Ron had a history of blacking out, and he supposed that Ron had blacked out while on the building site and had fallen headfirst to the concrete. David knew that the best thing he could do, and the thing that Ron would have wanted him to do, was to carry on and finish building the new church.

David was soon wondering whether finishing the project would be possible. The men refused to show up on the job site. Every Balinese person knew that the area around Blimbingsari was the place of the evil spirits (which is why the location had originally been called Alas Rangda), and it was obvious to the men that an evil spirit inhabited the building site.

How else could such a thing have happened to Ron? If there was an evil spirit on the job site, the workers would not return to work.

Each morning David got up and went to work on the new church. He worked alone, hoping that his example would encourage the men to come back to the job. But after two weeks no one had shown up to work, and David was beginning to wonder whether the men would ever come back. At this rate it would take him many years to finish the project by himself.

Chapter 11

The Reality of Poverty

D o you need some help?"

David looked down from the scaffold he was standing on to see Made Wenton, a young man from the neighboring Hindu village. He climbed down and talked to Made, who explained that he wanted to earn some money and had heard that David desperately needed help on the building job in Blimbingsari. David put the young man straight to work.

The sight of Made Wenton working with David on the church building site had an impact on the village. Slowly over the next several days, men began showing up to work at the site, and things got back into full swing. David was relieved—and surprised that a Hindu had shown the Christians that they had nothing to be afraid of.

The water that now flowed down from the dam into the village was beginning to impact the community. Until now the people had lived at a subsistence level. Being dependent as they were on the seasonal rains to nourish the seedlings they planted, they were able to grow only one crop a year on their land. And if the rains were late coming, it meant that they could not grow a crop that year. But now, with an ample water supply, they were able to irrigate their fields whether the rains came or not. Better yet, instead of growing one crop a year, they could now grow two crops a year.

Despite the improvement the water supply had brought to the economics of the village, David was concerned about the level of poverty that still pervaded the community and, as he had noted on his trips to Java, was pervasive throughout most of Indonesia. As he talked to people in the village and closely watched how they went about things, he began to see that this poverty arose not because people were lazy—far from it. The Indonesian people he observed were incredibly hard working. Rather, people were born into poverty with no opportunity to ever rise above it. The problem arose because most people did not own the land on which they grew their crops. Instead, they were tenant farmers, who turned over the greater share of their crop to the landowner in return for being allowed to farm the land. If a farmer gave 60 percent of his crop to the landowner, he was left with 40 percent with which to feed his family. And since he could grow a crop only once a year, there was a period each year when the fields were fallow and not producing anything.

To tide them over during these periods, the tenant farmers would borrow money from the landowner, who in turn took a greater percentage of their crop to pay the money back. Over time this approach snowballed into massive indebtedness, where the debt owed to the landowner was passed from one generation to the next. As a result, when a child was born into a tenant-farming family, that child was already in debt to the landowner, with no way of ever breaking the cycle. Instead, the child would work for the landowner, possibly in a factory, or struggle along through life and pass on more debt to his or her children.

Obviously, being able to now grow two crops a year was going to help some, but it wasn't going to break the cycle. Something else was needed. People needed a way to break out and stay out of the cycle. David knew that simply granting money to farmers to pay off their debts was not the answer. Yes, it got the farmers free of debt, but it provided no mechanism for them to stay out of it, and before long they would be back where they started—ensnared in debt.

In the evenings when the girls had gone to bed, David and Carol would sit by the light of a kerosene lantern and discuss the whole issue of poverty, seeking to understand its nature more deeply and come up with solutions to it.

Then one day as David was on his way to supervise work at one of the building sites in the village,

Ketut Suwira excitedly stopped David and told him the good news that his wife was pregnant. David's mind immediately drifted to the debt that the child would inherit, and after congratulating Ketut Suwira on his wife's pregnancy, David asked, "What could you do with your spare time to make some money?"

Ketut Suwira had not been anticipating the question, and he had to think for a few moments. Eventually he replied, "My wife is very good at sewing."

Ketut Suwira talked with David about the kinds of things his wife sewed and what she would need so that she could do more sewing. Before long the two men had come up with a plan. David would buy Ketut Suwira's wife a new sewing machine with which she would sew dresses, and then Ketut Suwira would sell the dresses to generate income for the family. Ketut Suwira was very excited.

"There's just one condition," David added. "I won't *give* you the money for the new sewing machine. I'll *loan* it to you, and you can pay me back a little at a time from the money you make from the dresses."

Ketut Suwira agreed to the terms, and soon his wife was busy sewing dresses, which he then sold throughout the surrounding area. Ketut Suwira was delighted with the income he was earning from the venture. No longer did he have to rely on loans from the landowner or moneylenders when times were lean. Now he was earning money that would help him and his family through those times. It wasn't long before Ketut Suwira had paid David back the money he had borrowed to purchase the sewing machine.

David talked to Wayan Mastra about the approach, and the bishop encouraged him to make more small loans. Wayan also told David that he knew of several others on Bali with impressive business plans but no money to put them into action. On Wayan's recommendation, David made loans—some of them for several thousand dollars—to these people. Among those he loaned money to was John Panca, who used the money to set up one of Bali's first travel agencies. David also continued to make smaller loans to the residents of Blimbingsari.

Each village in Bali had its own unique hierarchy, and Blimbingsari was no different. David was aware of this and did not want to upset that hierarchy by being seen to play favorites with people in the village, loaning money to some and not to others. Thus the loans he made to people in the village were made after consultation with the village elders. When a person received a loan, as far as he or she knew, the money came not from David but from the Bali church.

Pak Nyoman Yusef, foreman on the construction projects, was an early recipient of one of the loans. When he wasn't working on the building site, Yusef would spend his time collecting coconuts. He would wander about through the surrounding countryside finding coconuts and loading them into his oxcart. Back in Blimbingsari he would shuck the coconuts to remove their fibrous outer skin and then stack the shucked coconuts in a huge pile behind his house. Then buyers would come from Melaya and purchase his coconuts and ship them to Java, where they would be turned into coconut oil. Of course, the buyers from Melaya would offer to pay Yusef only a small portion of what his coconuts were actually worth, but there was not much Yusef could do about the situation. He needed the money, and if he didn't take their price, how was he going to get the coconuts to the factories in Java to sell?

David smiled to himself when he saw the look of joy that spread across Pak Nyoman Yusef's face when he received his thousand-dollar loan. With the money in hand, Yusef headed to Denpasar and arrived back driving a small truck. With a smile he showed David the truck, explaining that while it was not new and was a little beaten up, it ran well and was perfect for his purposes. The high wooden sides on the back meant that he could pile the back of the truck high with coconuts. He explained that there were far more coconuts to be collected around the area than he could ever fit on his oxcart. With the truck he could now collect these coconuts. And with the truck he could also transport them himself by ferry to Java, where he could get more money when he sold them. Soon Yusef had collected so many coconuts that he needed to employ other men in the village to help him shuck and prepare them for transport to Java.

David was delighted to see the way the loan had changed Yusef's economic outlook as well as the economic outlook of the men Yusef was now employing. No longer did these men need to rely on landowners and moneylenders when times were financially tight, since they were now earning their own income.

People outside the village began to notice the changes taking place in Blimbingsari. Officials from other aid agencies working in Indonesia visited the place to see firsthand what David had been able to achieve. They questioned David as to how they might be able to replicate in the places they were working what he had done in the village. David was glad to pass on his insights to them. The Indonesian government also took note of the changes taking place in Blimbingsari. They were so impressed with the economic change taking place there that they had a new access road to the village built, complete with bridges over the deepest ravines. And when electric power finally made it to the area, Blimbingsari was the first village hooked up to the grid.

Finally David's part of the construction of the new church was done. It was now time for Balinese artisans to carve the stone and wood panels that would adorn the new church's walls and to thatch and install the structure's traditional roof. With his part done, David knew that it was time for him and his family to move on from Blimbingsari. They decided to return to Sydney but only for a short time. David had already agreed to come back to Bali and help Wayan Mastra develop a training school in the Kuta Beach area to train workers for the blossoming tourist industry.

It was not easy for the Bussaus to leave Blimbingsari. They had grown attached to both the people and the place. David's vision and development skills had left their mark on the village and on the lives of its residents, and the village in turn had left its mark on David. Just before Christmas 1977, after the Bussaus had been in Blimbingsari for a year, the entire village turned out to wish David, Carol, and the girls farewell as they set out for Denpasar and a flight back to Sydney. Leigh Coleman had decided to stay behind in the village and help supervise the finishing touches on some of the projects.

Back in Sydney, David renewed relationships with people, who were anxious to hear about his time in Bali. It was good to once again be sitting in a pew at Waverly Methodist Mission. But as much as it was nice to be back in Australia, David kept focused on the reason he was home—to set things in order financially for the future. While he had been in Bali, the sale of his construction companies had been finalized. The only business that tied him to that phase of his life was the tile and bathroom store in Rose Bay, which he also decided to sell.

David wanted to be free to pursue what he now saw as his life's calling—using his entrepreneurial business skills to help poor and underprivileged people. To this end David and Carol set up a trust, which they called Maranatha Trust, into which they moved all of their assets except their house on Darley Road. Money from the trust would then support the Bussau family in their full-time ministry and provide seed money to allow them to continue making loans to the poor. The investment climate at the time was yielding high rates of return, and from its inception the trust began to prosper, making even more money available for the Bussaus' ministry.

While back in Sydney, David collaborated with his friend Garry Cairncross, a draftsman, and the two of them came up with detailed plans for the new training school in Bali. Once they were satisfied with the plans, David forwarded them on to Wayan Mastra for his perusal and approval.

While in Sydney, David also set about securing a more permanent visa for Indonesia. This was not easy to obtain, and during their time in Blimbingsari the Bussau family had stayed in Bali on tourist visas, which had to be renewed every thirty days. However, every ninety days they were forced to leave Indonesia, travel to Singapore, and then reenter the country to secure a new tourist visa. The situation was frustrating for David, who wanted to be done with the constant hassle of renewing temporary visas. It took a little while—Indonesian bureaucracy moved slowly—and there was much paperwork, but eventually visas were issued for the family.

After a year back in Australia, David, Carol, and the girls climbed aboard an airplane in Sydney, once again bound for Bali and the next chapter of their lives.

Chapter 12

A Growing Reputation

David was glad to be back in Bali. The place was beginning to feel like home to him. David and Carol and the girls settled into a newly built cottage on thirty acres of land in the Kuta Beach, Seminyak area. Wayan Mastra had acquired the land on which to build Dhyana Pura, a hotel training school. Once he had settled in, David got to work supervising the building of the training center. It was a big job, and it kept him busy. Hotel rooms, a restaurant, conference hall, reception and administration building, and maintenance facilities as well as training facilities all had to be built, and then the grounds needed to be landscaped.

Wayan Mastra's plan was to operate the facility as a guest hotel and conference center for the Bali

Christian Church. Students in the hotel training school would staff the hotel so that they could right away put to work the skills they were learning in the classrooms. Once a student had become proficient in a particular skill, he or she would then be able to secure a job that paid well in one of the new hotels that were popping up along Bali's white-sand beaches. These hotels were growing fast as more and more tourists from Australia, New Zealand, and Europe began coming to Bali to enjoy its beaches, take in the magnificent scenery of the island, and bask in the warm, tropical sunshine. Before long David was supervising the finishing touches to the facility, and Dhyana Pura was soon ready for guests and students.

The students were drawn from Bali's economically disadvantaged outlying villages, and soon their excited voices filled the grounds of Dhyana Pura. Among them were Ketut Suweria, who served as office manager; Ketut Wasiata, their house girl from Blimbingsari, who had come to train as a kitchen supervisor; and Made Wenton, who had worked with David following Ron Hewitt's death when the other workers would not return to the job site. Made had converted to Christianity and now wanted to become an electrician.

With the arrival of students at the hotel training school, it was time for David to switch gears from supervising the building of the school to managing Dhyana Pura. His first job was to set up the various training programs, and there was a lot to teach the students. Carol stepped in to help. She found herself teaching those students training to work in house-keeping how to clean a room to the standards Western guests expected. Training them to clean bathrooms was a particular challenge, since most of the students came from homes in the villages that had outhouses rather than bathrooms. They had to learn how to clean and disinfect a bathroom thoroughly, and especially not to use the same cloth they had used for wiping down the toilet to wipe down the basin and shower.

Carol also came up with a menu for the restaurant that balanced Balinese culinary delights with Western staples. Then she and David began to teach those students who wanted to become cooks how to prepare the ingredients, cook the various menu items, and present them on a plate. Carol also taught the students English so that they could communicate proficiently with Western guests.

Meanwhile, David was teaching students everything from gardening and managing the hotel front desk to various aspects of maintenance, such as carpentry, electrical, and plumbing. He also taught them the importance of being on time for work and getting things done on time. It was not unusual for him to have to go some mornings and rouse students from their beds so that they would be on time for class at the training center.

It was a busy time for both David and Carol, but eventually the students had learned enough to get the place running. Soon retreats were being held at Dhyana Pura, and guests were staying in the hotel rooms and eating in the restaurant.

While the hotel training school took much of his time, David was also kept busy in other areas. He was still involved in making small loans to people, and he was overseeing several small building projects going on in Blimbingsari. And while the Bussaus had been back in Australia, Wayan Mastra had drawn up development plans for many other villages throughout Bali and had since asked David to supervise these ambitious projects.

One of the things the bishop wanted was a water supply system set up in his home village of Sibetan like the one at Blimbingsari. David decided to bring Leigh Coleman in on this project, and the two of them set out for Sibetan on their motorcycles to investigate how best to go about it. The track that wound up the side of Mount Agung to the village was so narrow that they were forced to leave their motorbikes behind and trek on foot to Sibetan. When they finally arrived, they found that the village was a desperately poor place made up of clusters of mud huts inhabited by undernourished people. But as poor as the inhabitants of Sibetan were, they treated David and Leigh to a special welcome meal.

As David and Leigh sat down to the meal, the village head explained that it was custom to share their delicacies with important guests. The greatest delicacy in Sibetan was the hormone sack from inside a dog's skull. David squirmed when he learned this, and he looked at Leigh, whose face had suddenly turned pale. Moments later the delicacy was placed before David and Leigh. David took a portion of the prized hormone sack and thanked his host for it. Then as calmly as possible he placed the jellylike substance in his mouth. It was slippery and rubbery as it rolled across his tongue, and then with determined effort David swallowed and felt it slide down his esophagus. All the while he showed no expression, and then he let a small smile spread across his face once he had swallowed. The smile was intended to send the message to his host that he had enjoyed their delicacy, but it was also a smile of relief that he had managed to swallow the hormone sack without gagging. He dared not look at Leigh to see his reaction.

Unfortunately for David and Leigh, the dessert that followed was also a local delicacy—a sweet custard made from the larvae of large spiders bred in the village to eat. Once again David steeled himself and then took a spoonful of custard. Once again he managed to get the food down and keep it down. After the meal he decided that the larvae custard was a preferable delicacy to the hormone sack of a dog.

In the morning David and Leigh were shown around the village. They discussed the best location to build a water supply system and finally came up with a plan for the project. Leigh agreed to live in Sibetan while he oversaw the building of the project. (David just hoped for Leigh's sake that dog hormone sack and spider larvae custard were not on the menu too often.) Meanwhile, David would return to Kuta Bay and oversee the development of water systems, along with building projects and road improvements, in other villages.

After Leigh had been in Sibetan four months, the water system was built and running. Leigh then returned to Kuta Beach, where he and David came up with another project idea. Motorcycles were quickly replacing oxcarts and bicycles as the main means of transportation in Bali. The trouble was that the Balinese were not very good at maintaining their motorcycles. David financed a repair shop nearby where Leigh, with his extensive background in motorcycles, would train young Balinese men to repair motorbikes. When a person Leigh had trained became proficient at motorcycle repair, David would loan him money to set up a repair shop of his own.

Soon after the repair shop was set up, Leigh confessed to David that the job was more challenging that he had first thought it would be. The whole concept of repair and maintenance was new to the Balinese, and the young trainees often made a mess of the simplest jobs Leigh assigned them. One day, when a young man managed to strip a thread on an engine he was fixing, Leigh lost his temper. He yelled in frustration at his understudies and picked up the engine and threw it out the window while the young Balinese men watched in stunned silence.

David continued to encourage Leigh. In time, he told him, the young men would understand, but for now the whole world of motorcycle mechanics was new to them, not something they had grown up around. Leigh went back to the classroom and persevered until the young men began to get the idea of motorcycle repair and maintenance. Before long, small motorcycle repair shops, a number of them financed by loans from David, were popping up around Bali.

Toward the end of 1979, a Sri Lankan man named Hillary de Alwis arrived to stay for a few days at Dhyana Pura. As he and David talked, the Sri Lankan confessed half jokingly that he had come to Bali to have a nervous breakdown. He explained that he was the Indonesian representative of the Institute for International Development Incorporated (IIDI), headquartered in Vienna, Virginia, just outside Washington, D.C. A man named Al Whittaker, who had been the chief executive of the Mennen Company, had founded the organization in 1971. As a Christian, Al had been deeply touched by the poverty he encountered on his travels for the Mennen Company, particularly in Latin America. Eventually he had felt challenged to do something about the conditions he saw, and he resigned from the company and started IIDI.

According to Hillary, Al felt that the real issue with poverty was that people needed jobs. IIDI thus set about forming joint ventures between American donors and businesspeople in Latin America, loaning them money to expand their business and in the process create jobs. Its first venture was in the nation of Colombia, where the organization had loaned money to a businessman who ran a tea and spice company. The man had been able to expand his business, create eleven new jobs, and repay the loan in two years. Based on the success of its first project, IIDI began similar ventures in other countries throughout Latin America.

IIDI had now decided to move beyond Latin America into Indonesia. With money provided by USAID (the U.S. government's aid body), it hoped to identify potential businessmen with whom to form joint ventures. But for IIDI and USAID to get visas to stay in the country, the Indonesian government had required them to undertake a number of development projects in Indonesia.

Hillary de Alwis had been dispatched to Indonesia as IIDI's representative. He had identified several businessmen and established joint ventures with them, loaning money for them to expand their businesses and create jobs. Hillary also explained to David how he had committed IIDI to several development projects—building a hospital and a school on the island of Sumatra and overseeing a large water project in Java. Unfortunately, Hillary didn't know much about development, and things were not going well for him on these projects. To make matters worse, several of the businessmen he had loaned money to were now reneging on paying back the loans. Hillary explained to David that he didn't know what to do next and thought that a few days in Bali might do him some good.

David listened patiently as Hillary unwound his tale of woe, stopping him to ask questions about the various projects and assess just how bad the situation was for him and IIDI. He quickly came to the conclusion that the situation was desperate.

David told Hillary that he had some knowledge of development projects. Over the next several days he took Hillary to Blimbingsari and to some of the other projects in Bali. Hillary seemed stunned by all David and Leigh had managed to accomplish in such a short time. And when David told him about the small-loans program, he watched as Hillary's jaw dropped. "I've never heard of anyone doing the same kind of work—making loans and overseeing development projects—that IIDI does," he confided in David. Before Hillary left to return to Jakarta, Indonesia's capital, David gave him some pointers on managing development projects and wished him well.

Several days later an American showed up at Dhyana Pura to see David. He introduced himself as Barry Harper and explained that he had just taken over as IIDI's executive director. David learned from Barry that when Hillary returned to Jakarta from Bali, he had called Barry in Virginia and told him there was a man in Bali he had to meet who not only was making successful loans to start small businesses but also had the skills to help IIDI with its development projects. Barry had made his way to Bali as fast as he could.

David showed Barry some of the development projects that had been undertaken in Bali. Then later, as Barry and David strolled together along Kuta Beach, Barry got right to the point. "Can you sort out this mess for us in Jakarta?" he asked David.

After talking about the projects for a while, David agreed to help and became a consultant for IIDI in

Indonesia. Soon after Barry left to return to the United States, David traveled to Jakarta to begin untangling IIDI's development projects. He talked with Hillary and met with government officials, architects, and engineers to straighten things out and get the projects moving forward. He then made repeated visits to the various project sites to check on their progress and give any needed technical advice.

With his work for IIDI, as well as the ongoing projects in Bali and running the hotel training school, David was busier than ever. He was relieved when Pak Sus took over managing the Dhyana Pura complex. Pak Sus was an able leader who had previously managed a large hotel and served as the head of catering for Garuda Airlines, Indonesia's national airline. David felt comfortable turning over control of the complex to him.

On some of his trips to Jakarta, David would sit in on meetings between Hillary de Alwis and the various Indonesian businessmen to whom IIDI had loaned money. The purpose of the meetings was to get the businessmen to start paying back the loans. Since Hillary spoke no Indonesian, he had to use a translator in the meetings. Although David spoke fluent Indonesian, he did not let on to the businessmen in the room that he could. Instead, he sat and listened to the conversations as they unfolded. From meeting to meeting the pattern was the same. The meetings were nothing but a hoax, and the translators were in cahoots with the businessmen, none of whom intended to pay back the borrowed money. David explained to Hillary that he was being scammed. The two men then came up with a different strategy for dealing with the businessmen, who slowly began to repay the money they owed, much to Hillary and IIDI's relief.

At the end of 1979, David met Al Whittaker. The two men had much in common. They were both motivated by their Christian faith to do what they were doing, and they held similar views as to dealing with poverty and working with the poor. They eventually came to an agreement that IIDI and David and Maranatha Trust would partner together on a number of development projects.

Back in Bali, David decided it was time to formalize the management of the small-loans program. The program had run fairly informally to this point, but as the number of loans began to grow, so too did the need for a better management structure. Together with the Bali Church, David set up Maha Bhoga Marga (MBM), which in Balinese means "The Way of Prosperity." MBM was an independent organization that would make and maintain small business loans to the Balinese. The organization had its own board, which David trained, and it was funded by a grant from IIDI and continued support from Maranatha Trust. Ibu Nyoman Yulia, a young woman from the Bali Christian Church, became MBM's first employee. She was hired to be the administrator of the loans program. Of course, hiring employees and administering the loans cost money, and to cover these costs it was decided that MBM would begin charging a minimal amount of interest on the loans it made.

David also tapped Priyadi Reksasiswaya, the son of Pak Sus, manager of Dhyana Pura, to be the manager of MBM. Over the next several months, David mentored Priyadi, teaching him all he would need to know about developing and setting up a small-loans program. David had learned that a process was involved before loans could be made to people. First you had to get to know a community, build trust, and identify the leaders among the people. Then you had to identify the needs of that community. Did the community need a clean-water supply so that the fields could be irrigated and crops grown? Or did it need an access road so that things produced in the community could be easily transported to market? Only when such issues had been addressed was it time to begin making small loans available to members of the community. And then it was important to identify those people who had an aptitude for business and would develop businesses that would create jobs for others in the community, thus magnifying the effect of the loan. Priyadi was a fast learner and proved to be an effective manager of MBM.

Among the first loans MBM made were to a number of small farmers to raise poultry to supply the ever-growing number of hotels and restaurants in Bali. Things went well for these farmers until a large poultry producer in Java flooded the Balinese market with bargain-priced chickens. Suddenly the economic viability of the small poultry operations in Bali was threatened, as was repayment of their loans to MBM. Concerned about the situation, Priyadi came to talk it over with David. As he thought about it, David knew that the Javanese producer could not continue selling chickens so cheaply in Bali for long. What the producer was doing was making a play for market share and hoping to drive the local producers out of business. The eventual answer to the problem, David knew, was outlasting the Javanese supplier, and so he set to work on a plan.

Hidden from public view at the rear of the Dhyana Pura property was an unused storage facility, beside which was a secluded space. On this space David built a chicken slaughterhouse and processing plant, and in the storage facility he installed huge freezers. The Balinese poultry farmers would bring their chickens to the slaughterhouse at Dhyana Pura to be killed and processed. The hotel would pay them for the chickens so that the farmers were able to pay back their loans to MBM, and then the processed chickens were flash frozen and stored in the large freezers.

Soon the freezers were bulging with thousands of frozen chickens. However, as David had predicted, the price of the Javanese chickens quickly began to rise, and when it reached a certain price, Dhyana Pura began selling frozen chickens in Bali. And because it had such a large stockpile of frozen chickens, it had an advantage over its competitor from Java. Now a hotel or restaurant could call and order a hundred chickens, which would be delivered within half an hour. This convenience alone allowed the Balinese poultry farmers to win back their market share. In fact, the approach worked so well that it continued as the way Balinese farmers got their poultry to market.

With all the development work David had undertaken in Indonesia, his reputation began to spread. Soon Christian aid agencies and relief organizations from around the world were calling him and asking him to come and consult with them on development projects they were planning or were undertaking. Before long David was traveling the world from Bali to advise on development projects or to bring under control a project that had gone awry.

David soon realized that it was not particularly easy to get to the rest of the world from Bali. The more he traveled, the more he began to think that he needed to be located someplace close to a major international airport. And, of course, he owned a house in Sydney that was located less than a half-hour drive from the airport.

David talked the situation over with Carol, and together they came to the conclusion that perhaps it was time for them to relocate back to Australia. David had just celebrated his fortieth birthday and had accomplished a lot in his life so far. But he knew that more and bigger things lay ahead for him. Besides, while David had done much during his time in Bali, most of what he had accomplished was now self-sustaining and did not need his constant input.

Eleven-year-old Natasha and nine-year-old Rachel were less than enthusiastic to be returning to Australia. Bali was home to them. They understood the Balinese culture, spoke fluent Indonesian, had lots of friends, and loved the life they led there. Indeed, David could see that the girls, particularly Natasha, thought of themselves as Indonesian. Despite the girls' protests, it was time for the Bussau family to head back to Australia.

A round of farewell functions in their honor followed the announcement that David and Carol were returning to Australia. David did not feel particularly comfortable at these events. He preferred to be working behind the scenes rather than have the limelight shining on him.

From Bali the family flew to Jakarta, where David had several meetings with Hillary de Alwis. Then in early January 1981, the family left Jakarta for Sydney. No sooner had their flight left the ground than Carol doubled up with pain. Her face turned white as the pain wrenched her body. "What's wrong?" David asked.

"I think it was something I ate at the tooth-filling ceremony before we left," Carol replied. "But I think the pain will pass soon."

The pain didn't pass, however, and after they reached Sydney and returned to their Darley Road home, Carol began to get delirious. Immediately David called for an ambulance to take Carol to the hospital, where her condition was diagnosed as hepatitis. The doctor explained that she must have contracted the disease from food prepared for her in Bali, and it would be some time before her strength would fully return. It was an unfortunate end to what had been one of the most exciting chapters in their lives so far, and neither David nor Carol let the disease cloud the affection they felt for Bali and the Balinese people.

David reflected on the change that had taken place in their lives from the first time the family left Sydney to go to Darwin. Back then he had been searching for some direction and larger meaning for his life. Now he had returned to Sydney certain of what that direction and meaning was. He believed that God had placed him on a path, and it was time to focus on the next step forward.

Chapter 13

An Expanding Ministry

As Carol regained her strength, David resumed his hectic schedule, traveling around the world to consult on various development projects. He also made several trips back to Bali to make sure that things were progressing well with MBM. Often he was gone for long periods of time, and when he was home, a flow of visitors came to the house to meet with David about upcoming projects.

While David enjoyed the challenge of helping other people and organizations around the world, he was always glad to return to Sydney to be with Carol and the girls. While home he would spend as much time with them as possible. Living back in Australia after Bali was a big adjustment for them all, especially the girls. After having been homeschooled by Carol during the time they had been away, Natasha and Rachel found it a challenge to fit back into a regular school in Australia. David did his best to encourage them through their transition. He also was deeply appreciative of the way Carol allowed him without complaint to travel and pursue his calling.

David continued to stay in close contact with Barry Harper and IIDI. The two men had forged a close friendship, and they would often talk together, brainstorming about possible development projects IIDI and Maranatha Trust could partner in. Then one day, several months after arriving back to live in Australia, David received a call from Barry, who explained that IIDI was considering expanding its work to the Philippines. "Would you be willing to work with us to transfer the leading method in Bali to the Philippines?" Barry asked.

Certain that this was the next step for him, David replied, "Sure. I'll meet you in Manila."

David met Barry in Manila in October 1981. It had been thirteen years since he and Carol had first visited the city on the way back from their time in Europe and Canada. Manila had been an overcrowded and poverty-ridden city then, and it was even more so now. The city's population had ballooned to over six million people, the rivers were so polluted that the water flowing in them was jet black, and diesel fumes choked the atmosphere, leaving a layer of soot on everything. You couldn't help but notice the squatters. Their ramshackle huts were all around, often butting up to the high concrete walls that surrounded the elaborate homes of the wealthy. Somehow the rich and the poor in the city coexisted side by side. Most of the squatters in the city were from outlying rural areas and had come to Manila seeking jobs and economic opportunities, but all they had found was poverty and squalor. These were the people to whom, if the project in the Philippines was successful, David and Barry hoped to provide resources so they could raise themselves out of poverty.

David and Barry began to meet with a number of influential church leaders and businesspeople in Manila. David could tell that many of these people were skeptical as he explained how the small-loans program worked. The leaders and businesspeople seemed even more skeptical when he told them that IIDI, in conjunction with USAID and Maranatha Trust, would donate three hundred thousand U.S. dollars to fund the project and another ninety thousand dollars over three years to cover the program's expenses, and that the funds did not need to be repaid.

Three hundred thousand dollars was a lot of money for an organization to give, and many of those he spoke to asked David questions to see whether there were strings attached. David explained that the only provision was that the money had to be used to make small business loans to the poor.

Questions arose about whether indeed the poor would pay the money back with interest. David explained that in Bali that had happened. Ninety-eight percent of those who had received loans paid them back, a figure that impressed many of the bankers and businesspeople David spoke to.

Still others questioned the whole notion of helping the poor by making small loans available to them to start businesses and climb out of poverty step by step. Nobody had taken this approach before. This was not the established way of dealing with the poor. Most often, aid organizations and churches would come and tell the poor what they needed to better themselves and then provide it. After all, weren't the greed and exploitative practices of businesses and entrepreneurs partly responsible for poverty?

The questions were not new to David, who had heard them all before from missionaries and those involved in development. These people had argued that what was needed was a redistribution of resources in the world, moving resources from rich countries to poor countries. David called this the "Robin Hood Approach" to development: taking from the rich and giving it to the poor. But as he pointed out, this approach was not working, and levels of poverty around the world were increasing. Instead, he argued, why not stop talking about wealth *redistribution* and start talking about wealth *creation*. Instead of accepting the notion that there was a finite pool of financial resources to be divided up and shared among the people of the world, why not just make the pool bigger through wealth-creation schemes, like the small-business-loans scheme? He would illustrate what he meant by recounting what had happened to poverty-stricken people in Bali when they were given access to resources (money) to help themselves. As a result of small loans and focused development projects, the change in the economic well-being of people in Bali had to be seen to be believed. David's persistence and patience in answering people's questions finally paid off, and a group of people decided to participate in and support the new approach.

Still, David had a few questions of his own about the scheme. In Bali the loan program had been conducted mainly in a rural setting in villages that had a clearly defined social structure. In the Philippines, however, the program participators would be working with people living in chaotic barrios in an urban setting. David, though, was sure that the model he had established in Bali would translate to the conditions in Manila and that any problems that arose could be solved along the way. Besides, it was important for the program's success that it adapt to conditions in the Philippines and that it have a distinct Filipino character.

In Manila an organization called Tulay Sa Pag-Unlad Incorporated was formed. In Tagalog the name means "Bridge to Progress," but soon everyone was referring to the organization as TSPI. David molded those who had committed to support the program into an effective board of directors. When he had done this, he brought Leigh Coleman to Manila to set up the lending and loan management systems, train staff, and identify and initiate the first programs.

In his time with him in Bali, David had watched Leigh blossom into a gifted worker in the field of development. Not only had Leigh learned how to effectively manage development projects, but also he understood all facets of the small-loans program, or microfinance, as it was now being referred to. And his easygoing personality and thoroughness made him perfect for the job in Manila.

With Leigh taking care of things in the Philippines, David resumed his busy travel schedule, stopping regularly in Manila to check in on how Leigh was doing and helping to solve any problems that had arisen as the microfinance scheme was shaped to conditions in the Philippines.

David also joined the board of directors of IIDI and began making regular trips to the United States to attend board meetings. The organization wanted to change the model it was using for lending in Latin America to the model David was using in Asia, and it wanted David's input at the highest levels of the organization as it did so.

When Cyclone Isaac slammed into the tiny Pacific Ocean nation of Tonga in 1982, the Australian Council of Churches asked David to go to Tonga and assess the situation and come up with suggestions as to how they could help the Tongans recover from the disaster. The thatched Tongan houses, or *fales*, had not been able to stand up to the onslaught of the cyclone-force winds. After visiting Tonga, David came up with a design for a new fale that was cheap and strong and would withstand a cyclone. He then oversaw a pilot program to build a hundred of the new fales in Tonga.

On one of his many trips, David met Vinay Samuel, a Cambridge University–trained Anglican theologian from Bangalore, India. The two men quickly became good friends, and before long Vinay had invited David to come to India and establish a microfinance program there. David and Vinay began to actively plan for this. As they talked things over, David learned that the Indian theologian had a dream—to start an institution where Christian leaders, particularly from non-Western countries, could come and study issues such as poverty and how to adapt church structures to local cultures. David and Vinay talked the issue over at length, and David gave Vinay much practical help in how to organize and run the institution in a sustainable way. As a result, in 1983 the Oxford Centre for Mission Studies opened for business in an abandoned nineteenth-century church in Oxford, England.

All the while David continued making regular trips back to Manila to check on things there, and he was impressed with the progress being made. Leigh had done a great job setting things up, and TSPI was busy making loans to enterprising poor people in Manila. Already small businesses were up and running, creating jobs and income for people in the barrios.

David also made trips back to Bali to check up on things there. Priyadi Reksasiswaya was doing a great job running MBM in Bali, and he and David were looking to set up similar programs in other parts of Indonesia.

Finally, in 1984, the time was right to begin setting up a microfinance scheme in India. David and Leigh traveled together to Bangalore and met with Vinay. Located in southern India, Bangalore was a large, overcrowded city, so overcrowded that the year before, the city government had forcibly removed a fifth of the city's population who lived in slums to an area outside the city, called Lingarajapuram. Vinay and his wife, Colleen, had then moved to Lingarajapuram to minister among the relocated poor people. Already Vinay had established a school for children whose parents could not afford to send them to regular schools. He had also established a children's home and a health clinic.

David was impressed with Vinay's practical approach to ministering to the poor. He was particularly moved when he visited the children's home. Here were children just like he had been—abandoned and considered by most to be at the bottom of the barrel in society. David knew how it felt to be in that position, yet he also knew that it was possible to rise above it and to shatter people's expectations about you. With love and care and education and access to resources, he hoped and prayed that the same might be true for these children in Lingarajapuram.

In Bangalore, David oversaw the establishment of The Bridge Foundation (TBF) to make and administer small business loans to the poor. As he had done in Manila, he helped to select and train both the board members on the new foundation and TBF's executive director, Paul Roby, a former squadron leader in the Indian Air Force. Once the foundation was set up and the board of directors installed, David left Leigh to help set up the loan programs and train the new staff in all the various facets of microfinance.

David would return to Bangalore every other month to check up on things and meet with Vinay Samuel. It was on one of these trips back to Bangalore that David was introduced to the poorest group of people he had ever met—rag pickers. The rag pickers were a group of boys, some of whom were only nine years old, who slept in drains or out in the open by night and who by day spent their time rummaging through rotting garbage wherever they could find it, searching for mostly scraps of paper and cardboard but also for plastic and metal that they could sell to be recycled. The boys took the collected paper to a small store, where it was baled and weighed, and they would be paid for it. With the money they would buy food for themselves.

James Solomon, a worker from a local Christian charity, pointed out to David that most of the time the boys were ripped off by the merchant, who always told them that the paper they had collected weighed far less than it actually did. During the monsoon season, when the paper became sodden and not fit to be sold, the rag pickers lived a precarious existence, stealing or searching for food amid the garbage to keep them alive. If that were not bad enough, the local police took advantage of the rag pickers, arresting them for minor offenses and taking the money they had made from collecting and selling paper.

James tried to help the rag pickers as best he could. He had set up his own paper collection center, where the paper was weighed honestly and the boys were paid a fair price for it. He had also started a small literacy program to teach those who wanted to learn to read and write, and he had plans to set up a shelter where the rag pickers could sleep at night. But all of this cost money, which James did not have.

David admired James's commitment and was moved by the plight of the rag pickers. In conjunction with Leigh Coleman and TBF, David and James came up with a plan to help the rag pickers. Their approach was two-pronged. They would financially support the setting up of an expanded literacy program, along with a health clinic, a shelter for the boys to sleep in at night, and a training program to teach the boys skills. They would also set up several collection centers and work to make them as profitable as possible so that the profit could be used to help sustain the project. It was hoped that the project would eventually become completely self-sustaining and the boys could run it themselves. David wrote a proposal for the project and found donors in Australia and Europe to support it.

David also then kept an eye on the rag-picker project on his many visits to Bangalore. Things were going well. James was doing a wonderful job with the boys. He had won their trust and confidence, and David was delighted when the first boy left the life of a scavenging rag picker and was able to get a paid job using the carpentry skills he had acquired in the training program. Other boys who were able to leave rag picking behind soon joined him.

If he thought the rag pickers were the most destitute group he had ever laid eyes on, David was in for a surprise when he visited Pakistan at the invitation of Michael Nazir-Ali, the Anglican bishop of Raiwind. Michael introduced David to the brick kiln workers who worked in the brick kilns scattered across Pakistan and occupied the lowest rung of society. The brick kiln workers were virtual slaves of the kiln owners, locked in by an endless cycle of debt. No matter how hard these people worked, they could never get ahead of the debt they owed to the kiln owners, who advanced them money to survive during the monsoon season when it was too wet to make bricks. During the dry times, each family of brick kiln workers was expected to make twelve hundred bricks a day. If they failed to make this quota—and they often did fail—they became even more indebted to the owner. Whole families lived in squalid thatched huts, and as soon as the sun came up each morning, the family would start making bricks and would not cease until the sun went down at night.

Michael Nazir-Ali took David to a kiln to see firsthand the brick kiln workers' plight. David watched entire families, from the youngest to the oldest, toil in 120-degree heat, seven days a week, digging clay, molding it into bricks, and laying the bricks out in the sun to bake dry. He watched as old men and women, too infirm to walk, were carried to the clay pit to lend their hands making bricks. For a family to make their brick quota, everyone had to help. David couldn't help but notice the despair etched into these people's faces. For them, life was nothing but agonizing toil. Michael told David that he was doing what he could to help these people, providing literacy programs for them and health care as well as warm clothes to wear on cold winter days. "But what else can we do? What's the long-term solution here?" he asked David.

This was a good question, and David didn't have an immediate answer. Yes, they could pay off a family's debt to the kiln owner, but then what was that family going to do? David pondered the situation, searching for a business solution to the problem. Finally he said, "Why don't we build our own brick kiln and let the workers work their way out of bondage. That could work as a long-term solution."

Soon a plan had been formulated. They would set up their own brick kiln on leased land, buy workers out of their debt, bring them to work at the new kiln, and provide them housing in a nearby village, where medical and educational facilities would also be available. For the next eighteen months the families would work to repay the money that had been paid over to buy them out of debt, and then they would be debt free. During that time, however, they would also get to keep 10 percent of the bricks they made so that at the end of eighteen months, each family would have enough bricks on hand to build themselves a house on the land in the village.

As he had done for the rag pickers, David wrote a proposal for the project and went in search of donors to fund it. He found a willing donor in the Australian Council of Churches. Soon David was making regular visits to Pakistan as well as to India to check in on the progress of the brick kiln project.

One thing the plan in Pakistan had not reckoned on was the backlash of the brick kiln owners. These owners had made comfortable lives for themselves through exploiting less-fortunate people in society, and they were not about to let that slip away from them. They began to harass and intimidate Michael Nazir-Ali. As time went on, their harassment escalated to threats against Michael's English wife, Valarie, and then to threats of kidnapping and killing their two sons, Chammi and Ross. Eventually Valarie took the two boys and went home to England while Michael stayed behind in Pakistan. David tried to help and support him in every way he could, but finally the threats against Michael became so great that he, too, was forced to flee Pakistan for England. Thankfully, Michael's departure did not mean the end of the brick kiln project, which carried on without him, much to David's relief and the kiln owners' chagrin.

When he was not in India or Pakistan, David continued traveling the world, overseeing the expansion of microfinance schemes. One place that was about to experience a rapid growth in the number of microfinance programs was the Philippines.

Chapter 14

Opportunity International

David was at home in Sydney on February 23, 1986, huddled over the television in the living room with Carol beside him, watching the extraordinary event playing out in the Philippines. Overnight, more than a million people had spilled out of their homes and into the streets of Manila, calling for the ouster of Philippine president Ferdinand Marcos and for him to be replaced by Corazon Aquino, the widow of opposition leader Benigno Aquino, who had been assassinated three years before. David was not surprised by the situation. It came on the heels of a closely contested presidential election, which Marcos had won, most people believed, fraudulently. David had seen firsthand the excesses and heavy-handedness of the Marcos regime, and he was not surprised that after laboring under it for so long, people were calling for change. He only hoped that things would go peacefully. And so far they were, with the army refusing to fire on the crowd in an attempt to restore order.

Things continued to go peacefully. By February 25, Marcos had fled to Hawaii, and the Philippines had a new president. One of the first things Corazon Aquino turned her attention to was eradicating poverty in the country. Aquino called for private enterprise to become involved in the process. Her call for help brought David to Manila, where TSPI was planning to take up the challenge by expanding throughout the country. David encouraged the TSPI board to follow the model he had used in setting up the organization: find committed Christian leaders and local businesspeople who understood their communities and form them into boards. Then the TSPI board should work with the boards for the new organizations to help them put lending programs into place that were tailored to their local situation. Before long a new partner organization, Kabalikat Para Sa Maunlad Na Buhay (KMBI), was operating in the Manila suburb of Valenzuela. Within two years, six more partner organizations had been established throughout the country.

At the same time David was traveling to Indonesia, where micro finance lending programs were expanding. Priyadi Reksasiswaya had already established lending partner organizations across Indonesia that were overseen by a new organization, Duta

Bina Buana (DBB), which David had helped establish as a national organization to service all the lending partners in the country. David was impressed with the work Priyadi was doing. He knew he had chosen well when he originally picked Priyadi to lead the small-loans program.

David continued his globetrotting ways, crisscrossing the world for weeks at a time. On some of his trips Carol accompanied him, and once a year he took Natasha and Rachel with him on one of the trips. He kept busy advising on development projects and overseeing the establishment of new lending partner organizations. With the growing number of partner organizations, more and more of his time went into encouraging the board members and workers in the field of these organizations. He also challenged them to seek new opportunities for reaching out to the poor.

David's trips often took him to Chicago, Illinois, where IIDI had moved its headquarters to from Vienna, Virginia. At one of the board meetings in late 1988 it was decided that, given the growth in the number of projects in which IIDI and Maranatha Trust were partners, the partnership should be given a name. The partnership of the two organizations from then on would be known as Opportunity International. Soon afterward, David split off from Maranatha Trust the part of the trust that funded microfinance projects and named it Maranatha Foundation. In time, Maranatha Foundation became known as Opportunity International Australia. Meanwhile, Maranatha

Trust continued to support David in his ministry and to fund such enterprises as church planting, evangelism, and educational programs.

After the name change, David set about forming Opportunity International partner organizations in Great Britain, Germany, France, Sweden, and Canada. The purpose of these organizations was to raise money for Opportunity International partners in developing countries, known as implementing partners, to be used to fund microfinance schemes around the world. While David was doing this, Leigh Coleman kept busy in Asia expanding Opportunity International's presence there.

With their various responsibilities within Opportunity International, David and Leigh did not get to travel together as much as they had in the past. David always looked forward to those times when his schedule brought him and Leigh together for a trip. One such trip was in 1990, when they traveled to India and Pakistan to meet with partner board members. When their meeting in Bangalore finished a day early, the two men decided to head straight to Lahore, Pakistan, and rest for a day before attending meetings there. They knew their time in Pakistan would not be easy. Things weren't going well for the lending partner, Alfalah, that they had established in Lahore. Alfalah, under the leadership of Younis Farhat, had actually been quite successful at making loans to poor women and investing in a preschool program, a health center, and literacy and vocational training for girls. The program made no distinction between those it helped, regardless of whether they were Christian or Muslim.

The trouble was that Alfalah's success had generated a lot of resentment and jealousy on the part of other groups. As had happened to Michael Nazir-Ali, these groups tried to scare and intimidate Younis Farhat. When that didn't prove effective, they began inundating the organization with frivolous lawsuits. This left Alfalah's staff so busy fighting in court that they didn't have time to collect loan payments from clients, thus causing the organization to lose money. David hoped that there was something he and Leigh could do to support Younis and the staff and board members of Alfalah, as well as to come up with a strategy to get the organization through this difficult time.

When they stepped off the plane in Lahore, however, a grim-faced board member from Alfalah met David and Leigh. "I tried to contact you to tell you not to come to Pakistan," he said after a brief greeting. "But you were already on your way." The man thrust a copy of a local newspaper into David's hand. "You cannot stay here. It is not safe for you. You must stay at a hotel tonight, and I will see that you get out on the first flight back to India tomorrow."

Surprised by the panicked tone of the board member's voice, David unfolded the newspaper. There on the front page were pictures of him and Leigh. Because David could not read the Urdu headline above their pictures or the text below, the board member quickly told him the gist of what it said. "Charges have been filed against you for antistate activities. The authorities plan to arrest you tomorrow when you arrive on the plane from Bangalore. Thankfully you have arrived early, and the authorities do not know you are in the country. This is to your advantage."

David and Leigh spent a sleepless night in a hotel room in Lahore, listening for any noise outside their room and half expecting the police to crash through the door and arrest them at any time. This did not happen, however, and soon after the sun came up, they headed back to the airport and booked themselves on the first flight back to India. As they waited in the departure lounge for the plane to board, the two men tried their best to blend into the mill of the other people waiting to board the flight. Armed military police were waiting on the other side of the thin wall that separated the departure lounge from the arrival hall to arrest David and Leigh, thinking they were on the airplane that had just touched down from Bangalore. Moments later, David and Leigh boarded their plane and were soon airborne and on their way back to India.

"I wonder if the military police have realized their mistake yet," David said.

"Probably," Leigh replied. "That was close. I did not want to spend time in a Pakistani jail."

"Me neither," David said with a deep sigh of relief.

This was the last trip David made to Pakistan. He was no longer welcome there. Not long afterward,

Younis Farhat was also forced to flee the country, leaving Alfalah to an uncertain future.

After the episode in Pakistan, David was glad to get back to Sydney, where Carol had good news for him. She had taken on the role of pastoral assistant to Les Cliff, the Uniting Church chaplain at nearby Prince of Wales and Prince Henry hospitals. David was excited for her. Carol had an innate ability to connect with people, especially when they were under severe stress. She had been involved in pastoral care at their local Methodist church, and David was amazed at the way she knew what gesture would mean the most to a person at a particular time. He knew she would make a wonderful assistant to Les Cliff.

At an Opportunity International board meeting in Chicago in late 1990, the organization decided to begin working in Africa. For much of the next year David was occupied in Africa helping to establish the first partner organization in the nation of Zimbabwe. In 1992 the new partner organization called Zambuko Trust, funded by Opportunity International, began making loans of up to three hundred dollars to poor people in Zimbabwe to establish small businesses. The program thrived, and soon microfinance programs were spreading to other African nations.

In June 1993, Carol's mother, Phyl, turned eighty years old. She was still sprightly, and for years she had lived alone in New Zealand. But now that she was eighty, she decided that it was time to move to Sydney and live with David and Carol. David was delighted to have her around. He had a soft spot for his mother-in-law, who arrived just in time for her granddaughter's wedding. On January 22, 1994, David escorted twenty-two-year-old Rachel down the aisle as she was married to a young man named Richard Ford. Ten months later he did the same for twenty-four-year-old Natasha when she married Adam Florence, an engineer for Qantas Airlines and two years her junior.

David was both happy and a little sad at his daughters' getting married. He was glad that Rachel and Natasha had both found nice young men to marry but sad that they would be moving out of the house to set up their own homes.

As soon as Natasha's wedding was over, David was on the move again. With the collapse of the Communist governments in the countries of Eastern Europe in the early 1990s, unprecedented opportunities were now unfolding for Opportunity International to set up microfinance programs. One such program was being set up in the city of Nizhni Novgorod, the fourth largest city in Russia. Opportunity International's director in Russia, Stacie Schrader, had invited David to come there and train the board members of the new partner organization, Vostmozhnost. To get to Nizhni Novgorod, David caught an overnight train from Moscow. He found his way to the four-bed sleeper on the train, stowed his bag on the rack above, and sat down. On the seat opposite him sat three grim-faced Russian men who stared coldly at him. David tried to communicate with the men, though it was not easy, since he spoke no Russian. But the men continued to sit grim-faced, their eyes burrowing into him.

As the journey progressed and the expression on the men's faces did not change, David began to feel nervous. Something was not right, though he couldn't quite put his finger on what it was. That was when he decided he should not sleep. Instead, he pulled the notes he had made for the training session from his scuffed briefcase and began going over them, all the while hoping that the three men would tire and fall asleep. But they did not. They just kept staring at him, and he decided that they were hoping he would fall asleep. Finally in the early hours of the morning, David had to leave the compartment to use the bathroom. He took his briefcase with him.

Upon his return to the compartment, David found that his bag on the rack above had been rummaged through and many articles of clothing were missing. And still the three men sat grim-faced staring at him. David found himself in an odd situation. It was obvious that the three men had robbed him, yet what could he say? He had no way of communicating with them. He thus was forced to sit for the rest of the journey with the men who had robbed him. He was relieved when the train finally reached Nizhni Novgorod and he could leave the carriage. This was not the first time David had been robbed in the course of his work. He had been robbed in Pakistan and Africa and three times in the Philippines, but this was the strangest robbery ever.

After spending a week training the new board members of Vostmozhnost, David was once again on the move, hoping that his few remaining items of clothing would not be stolen on the return trip to Moscow.

By 1996 Opportunity International was growing rapidly. The organization now had fifty-seven partner organizations working in twenty-seven countries and making over one hundred thousand loans per year. Things had come a long way from the first small loans David had made back in Blimbingsari nineteen years before.

As the explosive growth within Opportunity International continued, the need for more structured management within the organization also grew. David understood this need, yet at the same time he personally struggled against it. He was an entrepreneur, and entrepreneurs did not fit well within highly structured organizations. Now instead of his being free to move about the world as he had done for so long, David was living under the watchful eye of the people within the organization who wanted to know where he was, what he was doing, and with whom he was meeting.

David chafed against this. He was a people person. His contribution to the organization now consisted mostly of nurturing the staff and board members of Opportunity International and its lending partners. He liked nothing better than to travel to a country and observe how things were progressing, listen to the staff's concerns, offer suggestions, and encourage and challenge the staff in the work they were doing. He also acted as their champion within Opportunity International, making sure that the voices of the partners working around the world were heard within the organization. This was work David loved and was good at. He was good at it because it flowed freely and spontaneously from him. But now he was being asked to confine his spontaneity to a box on a management flowchart and account for what he was doing. As a result, the work David had loved for so many years was becoming frustrating to him, and he tried as much as possible to resist being pigeonholed into a management structure.

By 1999 a new challenge had presented itself to David, and he threw himself into meeting it. When David had started making small loans to poor people as a means to help them climb out of poverty, those working within the development field had resisted the notion. David himself had taken to calling himself the black sheep of the development world because of the unpopularity of his ideas. But in the twenty-two years since making his first small loans in Bali, things had changed drastically. David was no longer the black sheep. The approach he had used was now accepted as one of the most effective ways to help the poor out of poverty. As a result, the concept had spread around the world, and all sorts of Christian organizations, aid agencies, and other nongovernmental organizations (NGOs) had set up microfinance programs or were planning to. David decided that these organizations and agencies needed training in how to efficiently set up microfinance programs to help the greatest number of people with their resources. He organized the first ever Christian Microenterprise Development Conference, held at the Ambassador Jomtien Hotel, in Pattaya, Thailand. Three hundred people attended, representing one hundred organizations and working in thirty-five countries. The conference was a huge success, with the participants coming away with lots of practical ideas that they could take back and apply to the microfinance programs they were running or planning to set up.

Following the conference David established the Wholistic Transformation Resource Center (WTRC) in Manila. The resource center would act as a clearinghouse for information and best practices related to microfinance programs and microenterprise development. The center began publishing informational books and pamphlets and offering consulting services to churches and organizations working in the field of microenterprise development. David also made plans to hold a second Christian Microenterprise Development Conference in 2001.

As a result of this new focus and challenge, David decided in 2000 that it was time for him to step out of active involvement in Opportunity International. He remained on the board of Opportunity International Australia and continued to support and raise funds for the organization. This was a big change for David. Despite the tensions David had felt within the organization over the past several years regarding his role, the staff and partners of Opportunity

International had become like family to him, and he would miss them.

Shortly after leaving active involvement in Opportunity International, on November 10, 2000, David was back in Sydney, gathered with some of his closest friends and his family to celebrate his sixtieth birthday. As he celebrated, David used the event not as an opportunity to look back at all he had accomplished in his life but as a time to look forward to a new chapter in his life and the new challenges it would bring. He was particularly looking forward to attending the next Christian Microenterprise Development Conference and helping other organizations become proficient in the field of microfinance and microeconomic development. He was also looking forward to being at home more with Carol and spending time with an ever-growing cadre of grandchildren. Both Rachel and Natasha had a son and a daughter each, and Natasha's third child was due the following month.

Chapter 15

New Challenges

The second Christian Microenterprise Development Conference was held in June 2001 in Pattaya, Thailand. This time five hundred people working in forty countries attended the conference. Throughout the conference David was kept busy. When he was not speaking to the gathered crowd, participants sought him out to talk to him or pepper him with questions about microfinance. David was delighted to have Priyadi Reksasiswaya as a speaker at the conference. Priyadi's knowledge of microeconomic development ran deep, and Priyadi was able to bring the perspective of a non-Westerner working in the field. David was impressed not only by Priyadi's performance at the conference but also by all Priyadi had been able to achieve in Indonesia. Sixteen lending partner organizations were now spread across Indonesia, and Priyadi had plans to extend farther.

Following the conference, Priyadi returned to Bali. David, Carol, Rachel, Natasha, and their families, whom David had brought with him to the conference, traveled on to Thailand's Krabi coastal region to vacation. Five days after the conference ended, while the Bussau clan was still vacationing at the beach in Thailand, David received a phone call from Bali. He could scarcely believe what he was hearing. Priyadi Reksasiswaya was dead. He had collapsed two days before in Bali, apparently from a minor stroke, from which he had been expected to recover. But two days later he died in the hospital of heart failure.

"We'll be there as soon as we can," a stunned David said before he hung up the phone.

The following day David and Carol arrived in Bali. Before setting out from Thailand, David had received the news from Australia that for his service to international development he had received the award of Member, general division, Order of Australia, in the Queen's Birthday Honours list. This was a high honor, and David could now put the letters *AM* after his name. But any excitement he may have felt at receiving the award was tempered by the death of his friend Priyadi. Bali would not be the same without him.

David and Carol attended the funeral services. David spoke at one of them, telling those in attendance, "Priyadi is not lost to us. His ideas and his spirit live on in the lives of the poor Indonesians he served and in those of you who have been motivated by him. His legacy will be passed on for many generations."

David continued to travel, consulting on microenterprise development projects, and made monthly treks to the offices of the Wholistic Transformation Resource Center in Manila to consult with staff. His trips were now shorter than they used to be. Where he had previously been gone from Sydney for up to eight weeks at a time, now he was usually gone for only three weeks at a time.

One of his trips took David through Singapore, where he met with Hugh Gollan at an Irish pub named Murphy's. Hugh was a New Zealander who had worked in New York, Moscow, and now Singapore. He was an expert in transitional economies—economies that were moving from being a centralized economy to a market economy, such as was taking place in the former Communist countries of Eastern Europe. Hugh was also a donor to Opportunity International. David found a kindred spirit in Hugh, and the two of them talked at length. In the course of their conversation, they talked about North Korea.

"Wouldn't it be great to start a microenterprise scheme in North Korea?" David asked as he and Hugh talked. Hugh agreed that it would be good, but both of them also agreed that they were probably thirty years away from North Korea being open enough for such a scheme.

Soon after his meeting with Hugh in Singapore, David found himself back in Bali. On the night of October 12, 2002, terrorists had exploded bombs in the Sari Club and Paddy's Bar, two of Kuta Beach's most popular nightspots. Two hundred two people had been killed in the blasts, eighty-eight of them Australians. The blasts had also devastated Bali's tourist industry along with the Balinese economy.

By the time David arrived in Bali at the end of October, barely a tourist was to be seen. David inspected the site of the bombings and talked with Balinese business owners, many of whose businesses had been funded by one of the lender partner organizations operating in Bali. The business owners were gloomy about the future and wondered whether their businesses would survive. David tried to encourage them as best he could. Bali was a beautiful place, and he was sure that it would not be long before tourists found their way back to the island. Certain that things would get better soon, David encouraged the owners to hang on in any way they could.

Back in Australia at the beginning of 2003, David read in the newspaper that at the invitation of the Australian government, a North Korean delegation was visiting Australia to study tertiary education. A public reception was to be held to meet the delegation. Recalling his conversation with Hugh Gollan several months before, David decided to attend the event. The reception itself turned out to be a rather tedious affair, but as he was leaving, David dropped his business card in the jar at the door.

To his surprise, a month later he received a letter from the North Korean government inviting him to North Korea to explore the possibility of cooperating on some economic programs. David again thought back to his conversation with Hugh. He and Hugh had thought it would take thirty years before such a thing was possible, but here, less than a year later, David was on his way with Hugh to North Korea.

David and Hugh arrived in Pyongyang, capital of the Democratic People's Republic of Korea (DPRK), to talk with government officials and assess the feasibility of operating in the DPRK. Before long they had entered into a contract with the DPRK government to set up a pilot project. Maranatha Trust would partner with DEFMOF, the Ministry of Finance, to set up a number of small enterprises. This was a unique situation. Since there was no private ownership in DPRK, all enterprises were state owned. However, each government department had an executive committee that could operate an enterprise. Maranatha Trust received applications for financing these enterprises, which in turn would generate revenue.

Hugh decided to quit his job in Singapore and came to the Democratic People's Republic of Korea to serve as CEO of the joint venture. When he later married, his wife joined him there.

At first, things did not go very well. Since the Ministry of Finance (DEFMOF) seemed more interested in accessing the capital that Maranatha Trust planned to invest in the projects than in growing the enterprises, they agreed to terminate the joint venture. Another government department was soon interested in partnering in the project, however, and things began to move ahead.

A new board of directors consisting of three Koreans and three Australians was formed for the venture, and soon small businesses were being financed— everything from poultry farming and shoemaking to producing plastic bags. Even a small factory was producing pharmaceutical products from urine. The manager of each enterprise was the person account-able to see that the loan used to grow the enterprise was repaid and that the enterprise ran profitably. As an enterprise ran profitably, more capital would be invested into it to expand and create more jobs. In this way, David and Hugh reasoned that the new jobs benefited the workers directly.

Of course, to many in the Western world the DPRK was perceived to be a dark and foreboding place ruled by Communist extremists who were not to be trusted. As a result, there were those who ques-tioned David's decision to enter into a joint venture with the government of the DPRK. But David saw things differently. He explained to those who ques-tioned his decision that there are basically two things you can do when confronted with a country like the DPRK. You can stand outside and throw rocks at it. That is, you can criticize the country and its rulers for their actions in the hope of shaming or pressur-ing them to change. Or you can get inside and do something about the situation. As far as David was concerned, throwing rocks at the DPRK hadn't done much to change things in the country. As a result, he had accepted the invitation and hoped that over time this enterprise approach would bring about the desired change anticipated for the nation.

While David was busy setting things up in the DPRK, back in Australia he was named Ernst & Young's Entrepreneur of the Year. In May 2004 he and Carol traveled to Monaco to represent Australia for the World Entrepreneur of the Year Award. He was the first social entrepreneur (a person who employs innovative solutions to address some of society's most pressing social problems) in Australia to receive this honor. While David did not win the title "World Entrepreneur of the Year," he was the first social entrepreneur initiated into the World Entrepreneur of the Year Academy, and he was kept busy while in Monaco answering questions and giving interviews to news organizations such as CNN and the BBC.

Instead of holding another worldwide Christian Microenterprise Development Conference, it was decided that it would be better to hold smaller regional conferences where issues related to a certain region or culture could be focused on. David kept busy traveling and speaking at conferences. By now he was an adept public speaker. But more than speaking at these conferences, David really enjoyed getting to know and personally encouraging the people who attended. Nurturing people was still the thing he liked to do most.

On Sunday, December 26, 2004, an earthquake in the ocean off the coast of the island of Sumatra in Indonesia sent an enormous tsunami crashing ashore in Aceh province on the northern tip of Sumatra, leveling almost everything in its path. After hitting Indonesia, the tsunami continued on, creating havoc and destruction in countries on the other side of the Indian Ocean. Banda Aceh, the capital city of Aceh province, was closest to the earthquake's epicenter and was almost completely obliterated by the tsunami. Early in 2005 David was invited to come to Banda Aceh to see what could be done to help those displaced by the disaster. Like so many other people, David had watched the disaster unfold on television news reports. As he soon discovered, however, the television images did not do justice to the magnitude of the destruction. As he explained, "Banda Aceh was the worst devastation I had ever seen in my life."

As he walked amid the destruction, David realized that what was needed most was new houses for people to live in. He quickly came up with a plan, which involved Opportunity International and a local NGO (nongovernmental organization). Basically they would set up factories to produce various building components for houses, such as roof trusses, windows, doors, bricks, roofing iron, concrete blocks, toilets, and sinks. The factories would employ displaced residents of Banda Aceh who were now living in tent cities, allowing them to earn a wage and wean themselves off foreign aid. The factories would then contract with various aid organizations such as Habitat for Humanity—which had raised large sums of money to rebuild houses—and would supply large quantities of building materials, for which the organizations would pay in advance. This would allow the factories to be self-sustaining from the outset. As well, the NGO proposed setting up a recycling program to sort through the debris and separate out sheets of roofing iron that could be straightened out and windows and doors that could be reused. These could then be sold as secondhand building materials.

The factories were quickly established and began production, and the NGO negotiated a contract with Habitat for Humanity and other housing organizations and foundations to purchase the building products they produced. In a matter of months, hundreds of people were being employed in the factories and the recycling program, and new houses were being constructed for the residents.

In 2006 David was extended another honor when he was invited to give the Australia Day address on January 24. Each year an eminent Australian is invited to address the nation, giving his or her unique perspective on issues such as the nation's identity and challenges confronting Australian society. David delivered his speech at the Conservatorium of Music in Sydney, and the address was broadcast live to the nation. David chose to talk on the topic of "A Giving Nation." In his speech he challenged Australians to think about who they were as a nation, to assess their place in the world, and, most important, to consider how they could make a difference in that place. He concluded the speech by saying, "There is a part of us that is designed to help others. Find that part. Create some space for it in your life. It's probably not going to be your whole life. But I guarantee you, when you get to the end of your story, you'll be glad you did."

In the course of his speech, David also uttered some words that sum up the course of his life so far. "Creative small-business people are the powerhouse of all communities, and more so in developing countries. The challenge is to release the incredible potential in human beings, to enable them to express their creativity and drive." For thirty-three years David Bussau has been committed to doing just that, working to help people release the potential within them—potential that can lift them even from the depths of poverty. And David is not finished yet.

When I, Geoff, flew into Sydney, Australia, in late March 2007 to interview David Bussau, I was a little apprehensive. I wasn't sure how the interview would go. In phone conversations with him, David had seemed a little reluctant to delve into his past. I guess I was not surprised. After all, the title of the 2004 book about David and the founding of Opportunity International by Philippa Tyndale was *Don't Look Back*. As I made my way to the Bussau home on Darley Road, I was not sure how things were going to turn out.

I shouldn't have worried. David was a warm and generous person who quickly put me at ease. Immediately I got the feeling that he was comfortable in his skin—aware of his strengths but also equally aware of his weaknesses. We sat together in the recreation room at the back of his house gazing out at his garden, and as I began to ask him questions, I knew instantly that my fears had been unfounded. Getting information from him for the book that Janet and I were about to write on his life was not at all difficult. Quite the opposite. When I asked questions—and I asked many—David generously answered them, often giving me far more information than the questions called for.

Our conversation was wide-ranging, starting with his childhood in New Zealand and moving systematically through his life. But it also took detours as David veered off to tell about Carol's ministry at the hospital, his grandchildren, his ninety-four-year-old mother-in-law, Phyl, who lived with them, and the garden we were gazing at. We talked about his deeply held Christian faith and how his Christian beliefs are fundamental to all that he does.

Perhaps the thing that struck me most during our time together was David's humility. I was sitting with a man who directly or indirectly had touched the lives of millions of poor people around the world. Yet if I hadn't know of some of his accomplishments ahead of time, I'm not sure that he would have bothered to enlighten me about them. The praise of men was not something that he seemed to relish. Instead, he was motivated by a driving passion to reach out and help others by using the entrepreneurial skills God has blessed him with. Having the freedom to do this was all he needed.

As we talked, I could see what was meant by "don't look back." The past is behind. It is what it is. All that remains is what is ahead and that is what David Bussau is focused on, open to every opportunity that comes his way to further his quest of the ultimate alleviation of poverty in our world.

When I asked him how he wanted to be known by people, his answer was fast and precise. "I want to be know as a social capitalist," he replied, "because

I am using capital and the marketplace to address poverty."

As we shook hands and parted company at the end of our time together, a breeze tousled David's silver hair. David's bright blue eyes shined, but they seemed to look past me to the next challenge before him. At sixty-seven, an age when most men are thinking of retirement, that is the farthest thing from David Bussau's mind. Instead, he is looking ahead, and the world will be a better place because of it. More important, poor people locked in the grip of poverty will have opportunities they never dreamed possible—all because David decided to quit his profitable businesses all those years ago and venture out in a step of faith, not knowing what lay ahead.

Geoff Benge

Bibliography

Tyndale, Philippa. *Don't Look Back: The David Bussau Story.* Crows Nest, Australia: Allen & Unwin, 2004.

About the Authors

Janet and Geoff Benge are a husband and wife writing team with more than thirty years of writing experience. Janet is a former elementary school teacher. Geoff holds a degree in history. Originally from New Zealand, the Benges spent ten years serving with Youth With A Mission. They have two daughters, Laura and Shannon, and an adopted son, Lito. They make their home in the Orlando, Florida, area.

Also from Janet and Geoff Benge...

More adventure-filled biographies for ages 10 to 100!

Christian Heroes: Then & Now

Gladys Aylward: The Adventure of a Lifetime • 978-1-57658-019-6
Nate Saint: On a Wing and a Prayer • 978-1-57658-017-2
Hudson Taylor: Deep in the Heart of China • 978-1-57658-016-5
Amy Carmichael: Rescuer of Precious Gems • 978-1-57658-018-9
Eric Liddell: Something Greater Than Gold • 978-1-57658-137-7
Corrie ten Boom: Keeper of the Angels' Den • 978-1-57658-136-0
William Carey: Obliged to Go • 978-1-57658-147-6
George Müller: Guardian of Bristol's Orphans • 978-1-57658-145-2
Jim Elliot: One Great Purpose • 978-1-57658-146-9
Mary Slessor: Forward into Calabar • 978-1-57658-148-3
David Livingstone: Africa's Trailblazer • 978-1-57658-153-7
Betty Greene: Wings to Serve • 978-1-57658-152-0
Adoniram Judson: Bound for Burma • 978-1-57658-161-2
Cameron Townsend: Good News in Every Language • 978-1-57658-164-3
Jonathan Goforth: An Open Door in China • 978-1-57658-174-2
Lottie Moon: Giving Her All for China • 978-1-57658-188-9
John Williams: Messenger of Peace • 978-1-57658-256-5
William Booth: Soup, Soap, and Salvation • 978-1-57658-258-9
Rowland Bingham: Into Africa's Interior • 978-1-57658-282-4
Ida Scudder: Healing Bodies, Touching Hearts • 978-1-57658-285-5
Wilfred Grenfell: Fisher of Men • 978-1-57658-292-3
Lillian Trasher: The Greatest Wonder in Egypt • 978-1-57658-305-0
Loren Cunningham: Into All the World • 978-1-57658-199-5
Florence Young: Mission Accomplished • 978-1-57658-313-5
Sundar Singh: Footprints Over the Mountains • 978-1-57658-318-0
C.T. Studd: No Retreat • 978-1-57658-288-6
Rachel Saint: A Star in the Jungle • 978-1-57658-337-1
Brother Andrew: God's Secret Agent • 978-1-57658-355-5
Clarence Jones: Mr. Radio • 978-1-57658-343-2
Count Zinzendorf: Firstfruit • 978-1-57658-262-6
John Wesley: The World His Parish • 978-1-57658-382-1
C. S. Lewis: Master Storyteller • 978-1-57658-385-2
David Bussau: Facing the World Head-on • 978-1-57658-415-6

Another exciting series from Janet and Geoff Benge!

Heroes of History

Also available:

Unit Study Curriculum Guides

Turn a great reading experience into an even greater
learning opportunity with a Unit Study Curriculum Guide.
Available for select Christian Heroes: Then & Now
and Heroes of History biographies.

Heroes for Young Readers

Written by Renee Taft Meloche • Illustrated by Bryan Pollard

Introduce younger children to the lives of these heroes with
rhyming text and captivating color illustrations!

**All of these series are available from YWAM Publishing
1-800-922-2143 / www.ywampublishing.com**